SOULGERY

Self-Surgery of The Soul

A Lifelong Guide to Unlocking Your Potential

Ahmet Bozer

ISBN 979-8-9985072-0-5 (print)
ISBN 979-8-9985072-1-2 (ebook)

Ahmet Bozer
Growth Colony, LLC
acbozer@growthcolony.com
www.soulgery.com

Production Management: Weaving Influence, Inc.
Cover and Interior Design: Rachel Royer
Copyediting: Meredith Mix
Typesetting: Lori Weidert
Proofreading: Keri Hales

To those who gifted me the freedom to chart my own course,
to the invisible currents that have guided me along the way,
and to all who seek to savor the taste of growth.

CONTENTS

• ACT 4 • HACK YOUR GROWTH

GROW FOREVER

ACKNOWLEDGMENTS

Years of working as an executive trained me to move fast, make decisions, and deliver results. I assumed writing *Soulgery* would follow the same pattern—a clear vision and a focused effort would lead to a finished product in a couple of years. Reality was far from that. Developing *Soulgery* turned out to be a marathon, complete with philosophical rabbit holes, surprise obstacles, and serendipitous discoveries. I finally finished it after eight years and eight thousand hours.

Though I stayed with it for all those years, this book wouldn't be what it is without those who encouraged, supported, and challenged me along the way. *Soulgery* is a product of countless interactions, moments of guidance, and the generosity of many who shaped it into something far richer than what I could have created alone. Words fall short in doing justice to their true contribution—one they may not fully realize, but that I feel and appreciate deeply.

My dear wife, Fatos, and I have been married for nearly 40 years. Living together for so long turns individual emotions into a shared undercurrent; you don't need words to feel each other's ups and downs—you feel them in real time. In developing *Soulgery,* the ups were intense, but downs were just as frequent. Throughout this journey, her support never wavered. As I have never felt its absence, I fear taking it for granted. I thank her from the bottom of my heart for standing by me and for sharing in this labor of love that brought *Soulgery* to life.

My children, Kerem and Esra, have been an unexpected yet continually inspiring source of wisdom—not just in the creation of *Soulgery* but throughout my life. Gaining deeper insight into their perspectives and benefiting from their diverse skills has been a true blessing. My late father, Ali Bozer, my mother, Nurten Bozer, my dear brothers Fevzi and Ömer Bozer have also helped me in more ways and more significantly than they may ever realize.

Sebastian van der Vegt, my longtime colleague and friend, played a pivotal role in this journey. When we began working together, I wasn't even a novice writer. Through his coaching I have grown into a more confident one. His sharp insights and relentless effort to elevate the quality of the content were key to me feeling as good as I do about *Soulgery.*

Sebastian also introduced me to his friend Frank Armstrong for professional editing. Frank's edits elevated the quality even further. Just as importantly, working with him made me feel that I had moved to a new level as a writer.

Having dedicated so much effort to developing *Soulgery*, I was determined to be just as diligent in launching it. In searching for a firm that could support me in all facets of the launch with a long-term approach, I found Weaving Influence. Working with them has been a rare privilege—being part of a team of experts who not only excel in their fields but also collaborate effectively and care genuinely.

I am deeply grateful to Aubrey Pastorek, my account executive; Elizabeth Mars, Laura Finch, Trenae Williams, and Franchesca Conner for their support in media relations; Isabel Thornton, for her gentle and inspiring support in building *Soulgery's* social media presence; Wendy Haan and Juliet Koubek for their meticulous and open-minded approach in developing the *Soulgery* logo and web-site; Rachel Royer, for her passion and creativity in design; Lori Weidert for flawlessly managing the book production process; Meredith Mix and Keri Hales for their sharp edits; and Molly Kellie for helping us feel like family when we had our meeting in Lambertville, Michigan.

This incredible team was led by Becky Robinson, founder and CEO of Weaving Influence, whose presence can be felt even when she's not around. I want to thank Becky for her authentic leadership and coaching. Last but not least, I want to thank Amy Driehorst, COO of Weaving Influence, who worked behind the scenes for a seamless experience.

As *Soulgery* is the culmination of my lifelong learning, I am grateful to countless individuals who have meaningfully contributed to its creation. To acknowledge them is to acknowledge the very fabric of *Soulgery* itself. My heartfelt thanks go to my extended family, my friends in the US, Türkiye, and around the world, as well as my colleagues from The Coca-Cola Company and the companies within the Coca-Cola bottling system. I am also grateful to those I have met in my post-executive life whose insights have enriched this journey—fellow board members, incredible teams of the businesses and NGO's I have served, as well as my mentees.

Finally, while this is a moment to acknowledge those who helped bring *Soulgery* to life, I know that books truly come alive through their readers. I thank you—the one holding this book—for making *Soulgery* a part of your growth journey.

1

THE SALT CEDAR

What human beings can be, they must be.[1]

—Abraham Maslow, *Motivation and Personality,* 1954

Salt cedars are remarkable trees. They thrive in arid climates and salty soils where most plants struggle to survive. Despite being invasive in certain environments, these tough trees with their feathery leaves and colorful flowers are a sight to behold.

I have developed an intimate relationship with one of these salt cedars on a beach that I frequently visit in Bodrum, a popular summer destination in Türkiye. Sitting under this tree, you avoid sunburn, yet comfortably absorb the sun as its rays seep through those feathery leaves. This tree stands only a few feet away from the shore, so in a southwesterly breeze, you feel refreshed as sprinkles from the Aegean Sea land on your skin.

My relationship with this salt cedar goes beyond those physical sensations. Whenever I am around it, a sense of calm takes over, as if nature itself is offering a moment to step away from the daily grind. In these quiet times, I often find my mind wandering to philosophical questions.

One of these questions has followed me for years: What really matters in life? For as long as I can remember, I have been a goal-driven person, setting targets for my work, family, and well-being. These goals provided direction and kept me motivated, yet they left me with a lingering void—a sense

[1]Adapted from the original quote, "What a man can be, he must be."

that something essential was missing. I could best describe it as the absence of an overarching goal in life. This void felt more pronounced as my intense focus on advancing in my career and developing as a leader began narrowing my perspective. During one salt cedar moment, as my mind flowed freely through philosophical deliberations, I came to truly understand that life must hold more than these pursuits. This awareness, in its quiet unfolding, revealed my paramount goal for life: to discover my potential as a human being—not merely as a business professional or leader.

Initially, I wasn't entirely sure what this broader idea of growth entailed. Despite this vagueness, I felt uplifted by a vision of a lifelong journey of self-discovery. My mind kept sifting through ideas about growth, but the more I tried to piece them together, the more elusive a cohesive narrative became. I quickly realized that I first needed to identify what was most fundamental to my growth, and then allow everything else to fall into place.

Around this same period, I became deeply intrigued by Sufism—a mystical path rooted in Islam. I was particularly intrigued with its concept of "transforming the *nafs*" to achieve a divine connection. As I delved deeper into this idea, a foundational theme for personal growth began to take shape.

In Sufi philosophy, *nafs* is considered one of the cornerstones of the human being. While definitions vary, it is generally understood as the inherent traits and tendencies of the self that hinder one's progress. Transforming the *nafs* is seen as a lifelong journey—dissolving these self-imposed barriers and gradually fostering a deeper connection with the divine.

I found this concept to be equally relevant and vital for personal growth, even outside a divine context. The essence of transforming the *nafs* lies in the ongoing work of refining the inner self—a process that involves deepening one's awareness of thoughts, emotions, and actions, laying a strong foundation for lasting growth.

The question I then grappled with was this: How does the *nafs* get in the way of our growth? A commonly understood explanation is that the *nafs* compels us to pursue earthly desires, often to our own detriment and at the expense of others. While I saw the merit in this perspective, I was more curious about the deeper psychological dynamics behind how we impose limitations on our own growth. Reflecting further, I began to suspect that the answer to my question lay in the sense of self—the thoughts we hold about ourselves. Shaped over a lifetime, these thoughts define what makes us unique, what we identify with, and how we judge ourselves. We clearly can't live without a sense of self, but could it also quietly inhibit our growth?

To clarify this suspicion, I decided to conduct an experiment: Could I become more aware of how my sense of self was holding me back, and learn to manage its influence? If I could, would this awareness meaningfully accelerate my growth?

The experiment required nothing more than setting aside time for meaningful self-reflection and remaining open to feedback. The timing was fortuitous. I was in my mid-forties—a phase marked by career stress, intensifying family obligations, emerging health concerns, and a deeper quest for fulfillment. Life itself provided no shortage of case studies.

Shortly after starting the experiment, I began noticing moments where my thoughts about myself were, indeed, holding me back. I realized this only after some introspection. At first, this limiting influence surfaced as counterproductive emotions: arrogance in disagreements, jealousy when comparing myself to others, or anger when receiving criticism. Reflecting deeply on these experiences through the lens of my sense of self, I finally came to see that they stemmed from an over-dependence on external recognition.

Over time, I came to describe this as an impulse to "serve" my sense of self—to preserve or elevate it—often without my awareness. Whenever this impulse took over, it clouded my psyche, distancing me from the task at hand and the people involved, fueling counterproductive emotions, and ultimately, hindering my performance.

Recognizing this, I challenged myself to control this impulse, even when I felt my identity was threatened. Could I replace it with a drive to accomplish something more meaningful? For example, could I focus exclusively on doing the right thing, or seeking truth, rather than serving my sense of self? My attempts yielded mixed results. In some cases, I managed to redirect my focus, leading to positive effects on my performance. In others, my sense of self continued to hold me back despite my best intentions. I share personal stories about these experiences throughout this book.

This experiment to understand the influence of my sense of self revealed three valuable insights. First, I understood that my sense of self holds me back whenever I give in to the impulse to serve it. Second, I learned that while this impulse may never be fully controlled, it can be kept in check. Each small victory, however incremental, contributes to meaningful progress.

Finally, I recognized the profound and far-reaching influence of my sense of self on my thoughts, emotions, and mental models. This awareness convinced me that managing its limiting effects is central to my growth. At last, I had identified the foundational theme of my journey and was ready to develop a model around it.

I realized that fully developing this model required space for reflection and experimentation. Stepping away from an executive role provided that space. During this phase of my professional life, I decided to take on different roles in business, non-governmental organizations, and academia, while also engaging in entrepreneurial ventures, philanthropy, and mentoring. The diversity of this portfolio offered even more case studies for refining the model.

Feeling compelled to share it more broadly, I envisioned the model as a flexible framework for understanding one's self and life that would be adaptable to individual needs rather than a dogmatic formula. I named this model *Soulgery,* inspired by the metaphor of performing "self-surgery" on one's soul to foster growth and transformation.

By this, I don't mean that we can directly "operate" on the soul itself, something I believe is beyond our reach. Instead, I see the soul as something we can only connect with. Our psyche—encompassing thoughts, emotions, and mental models—plays a vital role in either obscuring or enhancing this connection. Therefore, the concept of self-surgery here refers to managing our psyche to cultivate a fuller human experience—one enriched by greater self-awareness, meaningful connections, and a sense of meaning.

SOULGERY

Soulgery defines growth as the lifelong journey of becoming an increasingly capable, impactful, and resilient person. Its fundamental assumption is that the keys to discovering our better selves exist inside us, but we are somehow distracted from recognizing them, or even from seeking them out. It guides the growth journey through a *Self Map,* a model which I developed to reflect the essence of being human, and what I call the *4 Acts of Growth*. These provide a comprehensive perspective on how we can leverage our real-life experiences to accelerate our development.

The 4 Acts constantly draw us into our depths, where we can find the keys to unlock our potential. They are based on four core beliefs about what makes the most significant difference to one's growth. These are:

1. Sourcing inspiration from life.
2. Focusing first on the impact we make.
3. Striving for performance excellence in all life roles.
4. Leveraging life's challenges for growth.

We will talk about the 4 Acts first in chapter 3 and then cover them throughout the book. The Self Map is fully explained in chapter 3.

In conversations with friends and family, a remark I often heard was how difficult it would be to achieve what Soulgery is asking of us. I agree that being honest about and ultimately changing one's self are among the hardest challenges in life. Yet, reassuringly, anyone motivated to do this kind of work gets progressively better at it. What matters isn't one's current capability but making consistent progress.

Two points deserve to be highlighted in this context. First, I acknowledge that the emphasis on working on our inner selves can at times feel overwhelming. Having said that, it is up to each of us to decide on the scope and pace of our journey to utilize Soulgery in the most productive way. We discuss this more in chapter 19, once we have covered all of the 4 Acts. Second, Soulgery requires a level of self-discipline, but it's less about following a strict regimen and more about maintaining a rhythm of engagement with it. Naturally, everyone's rhythm will be unique.

Soulgery accelerates growth as a natural consequence of our experiences. As a flexible model, it empowers us to chart our own course, assess our progress, and make adjustments to keep moving forward. It will help us grow like salt cedars. Just as they have deep root systems which tap into ground water sources and an ability to adapt to salt, working with Soulgery helps lay deep roots within ourselves so that we can thrive in challenging environments. However, there is one crucial difference.

The salt cedars are very domineering trees. As their deep roots monopolize the ground water sources and they discharge salt into the soil, they make it almost impossible for other species to survive around them. Soulgery does just the opposite. It will help us engage with our human ecosystem in a mutually beneficial way.

THE JOY OF GROWTH

A lifelong journey of growth will help us discover more of our untapped potential, bringing rewards in terms of real-life outcomes. The growth experience itself is no less rewarding. Among its many joys, what stands out for me are two apparent paradoxes.

The first is a simultaneous feeling of amazement and normalcy. You are often amazed at the difference between your current self and a previous version that has receded into the distance; but at the same time, it feels normal because you have evolved naturally to that point. The other feeling is one of fulfillment and a drive to keep moving forward. You feel contented and paradoxically, that contentment becomes a driving force to do more and to discover more about yourself.

Personal growth has always been important. Now that the technological revolution of our times seems to be taking us into a more uncertain future, it has become critical. This new phase unfolding before us is demanding we step up our game in our own growth like no other period in history. The next chapter makes the case for that.

2

AGE OF DISCOVERY II

The future is not some place we are going but one we are creating. The paths to it are not found but made, and the activity of making them changes both the maker and the destination.

—John Schaar, *Legitimacy in the Modern State,* 1981

Throughout history, humanity has continually transitioned from one era to the next—spanning from ancient civilizations to the modern age. Today, we appear to be in the midst of yet another profound shift. Invariably, each new era feels unprecedented as it comes into being, and the same can be said of this one—although a few of its characteristics set it apart.

We have never seen so many technologies develop at such an exponential rate. Whether it is generative artificial intelligence, genomics, neuroscience, or satellite networks, each one of these technologies can transform our lives on their own. Others like blockchain, quantum computing, and virtual reality are no different. The convergence of these technologies is making this transformation more radical.

Around the world, massive amounts of capital and human resources are being deployed behind these technologies. The entrepreneurial energy behind them is creating products and services which change the way we work, shop, entertain, and learn. That energy is also being directed at solving some of the more pressing problems of our times such as environmental sustainability, agriculture, energy, health care, and transportation.

The impact of this technological revolution at a societal and global level has been debated intensely. There is no question in my mind that this is the most remarkable transition in human history. However, it is neither a road to Armageddon, nor the onset of our collective Nirvana.

Among all the radical changes we can expect in our lives, the most daunting one for me—even more than machines taking away our jobs—is how this new era can rattle us to our core. Feeling a connection with our human essence has always been a challenge. This technological revolution is making that even more difficult. Let's unpack this.

First of all, boundaries of *reality* are becoming increasingly blurred. Quantum mechanics had already reshaped our understanding of reality, though its effects rarely reached everyday life. Now, however, the rise of virtual, augmented, or mixed realities will impact our experiences directly. Compounding this, constant manipulation from external influences and AI-generated content can further cloud our grasp on what's real.

Second, our *usefulness* is being called into question. Today, machines can beat us in performing many physical tasks. We have not only grown used to that but enjoy it. Machines can also beat us at many intellectual tasks, and, over time, they will beat us in even more. As they become better at recognizing and responding to our emotions, they will further undermine our relevance.

Finally, a notable increase in *life expectancy* seems to be in sight. We may be moving from where we are today—70s on average globally—to 120s. A long life, with a blurred sense of reality, and a feeling of diminishing usefulness could be quite tiring.

As this new era is challenging our very core, it is time that we build ourselves from within. I am convinced that cultivating a strong inner self will have a far greater impact over our lives than even the most radical changes brought about by this technological revolution.

I witnessed the importance of having a strong core—albeit, in relation to physical structures, rather than human beings—during the 1999 earthquake in the Marmara region of Türkiye. Visiting the impacted areas shortly afterwards, it was striking to see completely destroyed buildings side-by-side with others that remained intact or sustained minimal damage. The difference lay in the way they were built. All experienced the same earthquake, on the same street, with drastically different outcomes. Tragically, the same pattern could be observed again in 2023 in the southeastern part of Türkiye, this time even more vividly.

In a way, we are like those physical structures. The stronger we build ourselves, the better we mitigate the risks and seize the opportunities posed by our environment. The keys to building that strength lie within ourselves, waiting to be discovered.

This technologically driven era brings an added urgency to uncover these keys. It is as if we are entering a second Age of Discovery. While the first one focused on exploring new continents and outer space, this new age calls for uncovering the richness of being human. Technology, far from being a threat to our lives, can serve as a powerful enabler of this journey.

As we advance on this path of self-discovery, the ripple effects of our growth will extend far beyond our own lives, ultimately helping to create a better world. A story by an unknown author about a scientist and his son speaks to this concept in a metaphorical way.

> *A scientist was at work when suddenly he was approached by his nine-year-old son, who was determined to help him. Preferring not to be interrupted, the scientist asked his son to go elsewhere for a while, but when he saw that he was not prepared to do so, looked for a task to keep the child busy.*
>
> *So, he tore a page from a booklet with the map of the world, cut it into small pieces, and gave it to the child with a roll of tape. "Do you like puzzles?" he asked. "If so, take this dismantled world map and see if you can fix it."*
>
> *He was confident the child would take many days to reassemble the map, but a few hours later, he heard his son's voice calling him, "Dad, I'm done, I put everything back together."*
>
> *At first, he did not believe his son. He thought it wasn't possible for a nine-year-old to reconstruct a map of the world that he had never seen before. Putting down his notes, he went to his son, sure that a mess awaited him. To his surprise, the map was perfectly ordered, and all the pieces were in place! "How*

did you do that??" the scientist asked his son. "How did you put the world back together?"

"Well, dad," the boy answered, "I don't know the map of the world, but when you tore the page from the magazine, I saw on the other side a picture of a person. When you gave me the world to fix, I tried but couldn't do it. Then I turned all the pieces around and started to fix the person. Once I fixed the person, I turned it over and saw the world had been fixed as well."

A lifelong journey of growth takes us beyond discovering our individual potential—it also helps shape our collective future. Every action we take for our own growth becomes a stepping stone on our "path to the future" as described by John Schaar at the beginning of this chapter. Paving this path transforms both "the traveler and the destination." Seen this way, growing ourselves is not only a personal endeavor but an act of contributing to the greater good.

Let's now explore Soulgery with a holistic view and embark on our unique journey of discovery and growth.

3

THE ENTERPRISE

A human being[1] is a mystery, it needs to be unraveled, and if your whole life is spent unraveling it, don't say that you have wasted time. I am studying that mystery because I want to be a human being.

—Fyodor Dostoevsky

Isn't it amazing that we can explain how galaxies were formed, yet we don't fully understand something as basic as why we yawn or have hiccups? We seem to have made better progress in understanding the universe than ourselves. This contrast becomes even more unsettling when we consider the vast mysteries still surrounding human existence.

From the mundane to the profound, we are constantly seeking answers to questions about who we are and why we are here. Is our life a time-bound experience on Earth or is there something beyond that? How did we come into being? Is there a Creator, are we the product of evolution, or could it be a combination of both? What about the role of fate in our lives? Do we truly have free

[1]The original quote is "Man is a mystery."

will? To borrow from Pierre Teilhard de Chardin: are we human beings having a spiritual experience or are we spiritual beings having a human experience?

The mysteries extend inward as well, into the endless stream of thoughts, emotions, and spiritual experiences that shape our lives in ways we don't fully comprehend, rendering human life a fertile ground for continual exploration. Through this process of self-discovery, we grow— not only becoming increasingly capable, impactful, and resilient, but also more human.

Soulgery serves as a guide on this journey. Its approach to the challenge of lifelong growth rests on a proposition for what it means to be human—*The Self Map.* We describe it fully here, an exercise much like introducing the characters in a play. The action part of this play lies in the 4 Acts of Growth—a comprehensive guide to accelerate our growth as a natural consequence of our experiences. We will provide an overview of the 4 Acts in this chapter and cover them in detail over the rest of this book.

The Soulgery model that appears on the following page includes The Self Map and the 4 Acts. This chart offers a holistic view, so you are not expected to fully grasp it at once. As you read this chapter, you will start to develop an understanding of the model and its components, with a more complete picture building as you progress through the book.

This lifelong journey of discovery and growth is both expansive and profound. The great Sufi mystic and poet Rumi hints at this when he says: "You are not a drop in the ocean, you are the ocean in a drop." We are indeed like oceans. Just as one dives deep into them to grasp precious pearls, we can find precious pieces of "self-wisdom" by diving deep into ourselves, paving the way to unlocking our potential. The Self Map is the map for that deep dive. Let's now submerge.

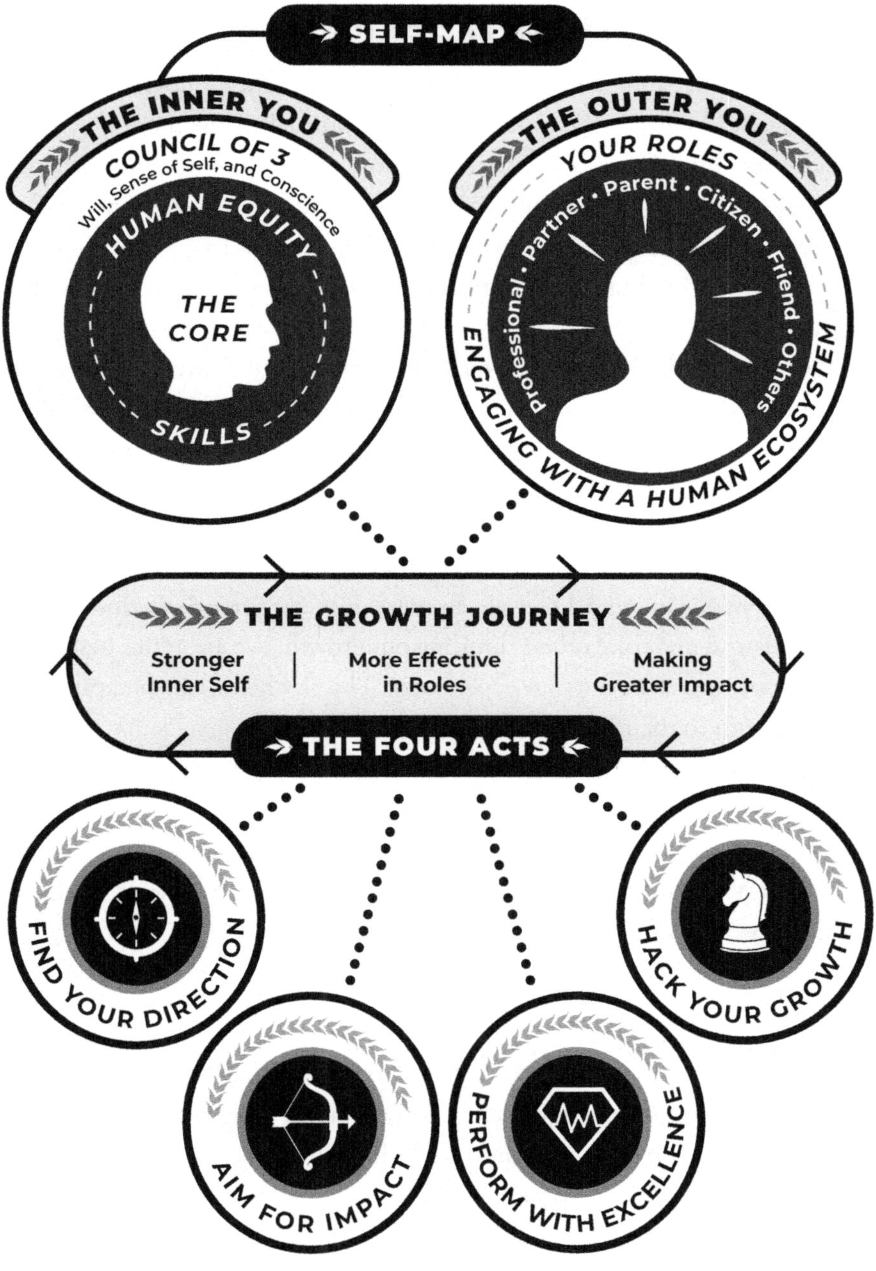

THE SOULGERY MODEL

OUR CORE: THE 4-D SELF

At our core, we are four-dimensional beings. We have the ability to experience life physically, intellectually, emotionally, and spiritually. The more we engage with all these dimensions, the richer and more meaningful our lives become. Yet, these dimensions often pull us in different directions, each asserting its presence. Sometimes our emotions lead us, while at other times our intellect prevails. A powerful desire in our physical dimension can dominate the others, creating imbalance.

Our spiritual dimension—the most mysterious of all—often fades into the background in this dynamic. Sufism and some other belief systems highlight this tension, suggesting that our mortal self tends to suffocate our eternal self. In other words, the more our bodies, hearts, and minds are absorbed in earthly matters, the more we silence our spirit. A profound opportunity for discovering our potential lies in learning to listen to its guidance.

This dynamic in our 4-D selves can cause us to consistently overuse certain dimensions and underuse others, limiting our growth. We are at our best when we bring our whole self into our experiences. This is when we inspire others by appealing both to their hearts and minds.

In his 1944 book *Psychology and Alchemy*, Carl Jung says, "Wholeness is not achieved by cutting off a portion of one's being, but by integration of the contraries." We can integrate the contraries within our 4-D selves by becoming intentional about using them. The 4 Acts will guide us in making this integration as we pursue our aspirations and navigate challenges. Over time, as we keep applying the 4 Acts, we will naturally reveal more of our whole selves.

OUR HUMAN EQUITY

In a materialistic context, equity refers to the value of an asset, such as a property or an ownership stake in a company. The more value we build into these assets, the wealthier we become. Similarly, we can cultivate intangible assets within ourselves. These include our wisdom, character, and the love we hold in our hearts. Collectively, we will refer to these as our human equity.

Our human equity shapes our desires, guides us in making judgments, setting expectations, and interpreting outcomes. It gives us a vision for life, and the resilience we need to realize that vision. The more value we build into our human equity, the further we will advance in our journey of discovery and growth. Acts 1 and 2 will talk about how we can enrich these uniquely human assets through our everyday experiences.

OUR SKILLS

Our skills are like tools in a toolbox. Some of them are specific to our line of work such as sales, engineering, or auditing. Others are more general, applying not only across professions and industries but also to our family lives and relationships. These include skills like communication, emotional intelligence, or collaboration, often referred to as soft skills. In today's work environment they are increasingly recognized as critical to success. Here we call them core skills, and strengthening them is a key part of our growth.

Applying the 4 Acts to real life will help us develop these skills in a natural way. Appendix 1 provides a list of the Soulgery core skills and how each connects with the 4 Acts.

ROLES AND OUR HUMAN ECOSYSTEM

We play many roles in life: as a professional, parent, partner, friend, or citizen. The world defines us in terms of our roles. I have been called "Ali Bozer's son" and "Coca-Cola Ahmet" at different stages in my life. It isn't hard for us to do the same to ourselves; defining who we are in terms of the collection of our life roles. We can, however, think of our roles beyond their influence on shaping our identity. They can be platforms on which we create our growth story. Each phase of our lives represents a different chapter of that story, shaped by the unique challenges we face and the determined pursuit of our aspirations.

In our life roles, we engage with a human ecosystem that includes our families, friends, colleagues, members of our communities, business partners, and others. Just as the ecosystems in which we exist impact our individual, economic, and social well-being, our human ecosystem also affects our well-being and growth. A healthy human ecosystem, rich with exchanges among its participants, lifts everyone up—whether a classroom, a group of friends, a department of a company, or a country.

We have a symbiotic relationship with our human ecosystem, where its vibrancy helps us grow, and our growth contributes to its vibrancy. The 4 Acts will guide us, in all our roles, to engage with our human ecosystem to fuel this mutually reinforcing cycle.

THE COUNCIL OF 3

Let's envision ourselves as an enterprise, containing everything we have discussed so far as its constituent parts. At the top of this enterprise sits the Council of 3—composed of our will, conscience, and sense of self.

Our will is the CEO of this enterprise. Just as the CEO of any company is critical to its growth, our will is critical to our own. It is what drives us to action and makes us go beyond our comfort zones. Our conscience is like a board member with the perfect moral compass, who tends to make comments in highly subtle ways. Honoré de Balzac calls it "the unerring judge until we stifle it." The will has an option to listen to the conscience, or not. When it does, it can guide the enterprise to do the right thing. When it chooses not to do so, the conscience is stifled.

The antagonist in this story is the sense of self. It is a powerful member of this council, which, if unchecked, will begin to dominate it. It has the potential to make the will exclusively work for itself and bury the conscience so deeply that no one can hear from it.

The Sense of Self

Our sense of self is the collection of thoughts we have about ourselves. These can come from how we identify with our nationality or religion, from sophisticated notions like the meaning we derive from a profession, or particular values we have embraced. They also include judgments about our self-image or self-worth.

We liken our sense of self to an antagonist because it can subtly and persistently draw our mental and emotional energy toward preserving or elevating itself. This distracts us from the task at hand or doing what's right. Every day, we see examples of how people serve their sense of self, often under the pretense of something else.

One of the boards I sat on had a dynamic where the main disagreements were almost always between the same two people. At one point, when the debate became more intense than usual, one of them got very annoyed, and asked why it was that this other board member always objected to *his* ideas.

Until that moment, I hadn't thought there was much going on in the conversation to warrant a personalization of this kind. To me, that board member asking that question clearly signaled his perception of an attack on his sense of self, prompting a need to defend it. From that point on, the discussion shifted, driven by his self-defense rather than by the issue at hand.

On reflection, I realized that this happens frequently—although it may not always be so easy to observe. This is because our tendency to serve our sense of self—preserving or elevating it—often becomes an unconscious mental habit. As it hardens through repetition, it keeps us increasingly preoccupied with ourselves, often to no useful end. This habit inhibits our growth; to the extent that our self-perceptions are flawed or misguided, this inhibition becomes more pronounced.

A flawed sense of self, along with the impulse to serve it, is an inherent part of being human. While it can be easily noticed in what we traditionally call "high-ego" individuals, it is present in everyone. Each of us has the opportunity to unlock more of our potential by managing its influence.

The far-reaching nature of our sense of self makes this an especially meaningful opportunity. The way we think about ourselves shapes how we observe, perceive, and engage with everything around us. This impact cascades into our decisions, influencing both the outcomes we face and how we process them. Said another way, our sense of self influences each and every part of the Self Map: our character; the ability to enrich our wisdom; our capacity to experience love; the strength of our core skills; and the way we engage with our human ecosystem.

We have two challenges to realizing this growth opportunity. First, the tendency to serve our sense of self often escapes our conscious awareness because it is almost automatic and emotionally charged, drawing away our focus in subtle, unrecognized ways.

Second, even when we become aware that we are driven by serving our sense of self, it isn't always easy to know whether this motive is inhibiting us. In fact, it can be argued that this drive is essential to achieving our goals. For instance, if we want our child to thrive—both for the child's well-being and to reassure ourselves that we are good parents—we can't necessarily say that the latter motive, serving our sense of self, has a limiting influence.

Similarly, at work, being driven by both a desire to make a difference for our stakeholders and a need to affirm our self-worth isn't necessarily inhibiting. The problem arises when serving our sense of self begins to dominate our psyche. Put simply, it's the "dose that makes the poison"—a phrase often attributed to Paracelsus, a Swiss physician and alchemist, emphasizing that toxicity is determined by the quantity of the substance. That is, a small amount will not kill you; it may even help you. But determining the right level isn't always easy. It can feel like differentiating between two shades of blue at twilight.

We can overcome these challenges through a conscious effort to become more aware of our own motives. These self-reflections involve making subtle distinctions between whether we have been serving our sense of self or focusing on doing what's right. Although we may not always assess ourselves correctly, the awareness we gain through these self-reflections will help us contain the limiting effects of our sense of self, eventually transforming it to a facilitator of growth.

Given the pervasive influence of our sense of self, we will discuss it in each of the 4 Acts. Throughout these discussions, I will share examples of how my sense of self has derailed me and how managing its influence has improved my performance. Reading these stories, it might seem to some that I am overly critical of myself in assessing my motives. That is probably true, but for a good reason. As this antagonist often remains under my awareness radar and can significantly inhibit my growth, I prefer to err on the side of caution.

Finally, it is also human nature for an inner voice to tell us that it isn't *me* with a flawed sense of self, or that *I* am not the one serving my sense of self in limiting ways. To unlock more of our potential, given the deep and far-reaching impact of our sense of self, it is best to be circumspect about that inner voice. It may well be the voice of this antagonist.

THE 4 ACTS OF GROWTH

Invariably, life will grow us in different ways even without these insights. The key is to maximize our growth so that we can realize as much of our potential as possible, to accelerate the rate at which we become more capable, impactful, and resilient. The 4 Acts of Growth provide a pathway to make that a natural part of our everyday lives. They mirror the core beliefs we shared in chapter 1 about what makes a significant difference to growing oneself. They are:

1. Find Your Direction: Sourcing inspiration from life.
2. Aim for Impact: Focusing first on the impact we make.
3. Perform with Excellence: Striving for performance excellence in all life roles.
4. Hack Your Growth: Leveraging life's challenges for growth.

Living by these beliefs requires capabilities that some might consider innate. Yet, the million-dollar question remains: are we born with our capabilities, or do we develop them? Embracing the 4 Acts will challenge us to achieve the latter, demonstrating that the progress we make in developing our capabilities is far more important than the starting point.

The first act—*Find Your Direction*—is based on the premise that we are more likely to feel inspired when love and wisdom flourish within us. Accordingly, it guides us on an inward journey to open our hearts and to harvest wisdom from our life experiences. From there, we are invited to the pinnacle of this journey: a search for meaning—a philosophical quest which transforms us from seekers of inspiration into its source. We cover the first act in chapters 4–6.

The second act—*Aim for Impact*—is founded on two beliefs: first, that the impact we make in our roles and our fulfillment in life are deeply intertwined; and second, that growth occurs naturally when we aim for impact. It presents the idea of "playing" our life roles with an impact orientation to realize our goals and to reach higher forms of fulfillment. Chapters 7–9 guide us to instill such an impact orientation within ourselves by embracing "a legacy mindset," and by cultivating human qualities which connect us to one another deeply and strongly.

The third act—*Perform with Excellence*—takes us from aiming to doing, with a focus on excellence in our "life performance." It steers us into finding our own rhythm for personal planning, managing time, and performing with impact. It also provides a perspective on how we can manage the well-being of our 4-D selves, as that is fundamental to our performance. The third act is covered in chapters 10–14.

Finally, the fourth one—*Hack Your Growth*—is about rising above our challenges to grow through them. It guides us to "read" our challenges in a constructive way, to respond—not react—to them, and to use them to "hack" our default modes. This is covered in chapters 15–18.

Each of us brings unique passions, strengths, challenges, and world views to our journey. The 4 Acts provide a guiding framework for thinking about ourselves and life—rather than a rigid recipe for growth—allowing us to chart our own course and progress at our own pace.

USING THE SOULGERY MODEL (SOMO)

Using SoMo is akin to how you might master the geography of a city with countless streets and neighborhoods. We can't absorb the map of the entire city with all its details at once. A better way is to get an overall picture first, and then to learn by enjoying the neighborhoods of interest. This chapter provides the overall picture for a growth journey. Reading the rest of the book will make that picture clearer. Ultimately, only when we apply these approaches to real life, do we internalize.

Applying Soulgery in real life occurs through self-reflection and insightful conversations. John Dewey, who is regarded as a pioneer of experiential learning, emphasized that true learning comes not merely from experience, but from reflecting on it. When it comes to personal growth, it is essential that the scope of our self-reflection encompasses not only what happens in our various roles, but also what unfolds within us.

We also learn through quality conversations: those in which we build on one another's ideas in meaningful ways, broadening our horizons, deepening our understanding, and developing an appreciation of one another. Having quality conversations as a part of our lives can make a significant difference to our growth.

The 4 Acts will foster holistic growth. An experience, for example, of landing a job, negotiating a contract, or improving a relationship touches many parts of the Self Map. As we reflect on ourselves in those experiences, following the Self Map and diving deep into ourselves when necessary, we will likely identify multiple opportunities for growth. By addressing them, we will improve ourselves on many fronts, moving our whole self forward with each testing experience.

Using SoMo should feel like ascending an upward spiral of growth and impact. Our core will become more vibrant, our human equity richer, and our skills stronger. This inner self will radiate through our life roles, making our impact ever more profound. Our human ecosystem will echo that impact, strengthening our drive to move forward and upward.

Rising through this spiral staircase, we will inevitably learn more about ourselves and life. The mysteries of life, however, persist. While they may sometimes be a source of disquiet, they also add a sense of enchantment to our lifelong journey. As the 18th century French writer Antoine de Rivarol said: "It is the dim haze of mystery that adds enchantment to pursuit."

ACT 1

FIND YOUR DIRECTION

4

THE SOURCE

Inspiration exists, but it has to find you working.

—Pablo Picasso

Picasso's words remind us that inspiration doesn't arrive uninvited—it appears when we immerse ourselves in action and purpose. Language alone struggles to convey the experience, yet ancient wisdom offers glimpses into its nature. A quote widely attributed to the Hindu mystic Patanjali begins to capture its essence:

> *When you are inspired by some great purpose, some extraordinary project, all your thoughts break their bonds. Your mind transcends limitations, your consciousness expands in every direction, and you find yourself in a new, great, and wonderful world. Dormant forces, faculties, and talents become alive, you discover yourself to be a greater person, by far than you ever dreamed yourself to be.*

Each one of us has likely experienced something similar. For me, one such moment occurred during a basketball game when I was 18 years old. It was the semifinal of the Turkish youth league championship. We had reached the semifinals undefeated, but this game was tough. We fell behind early on and trailed by 20 points for most of the game. It felt like a lost cause, but then, around the middle of the second half, the tide began to turn. We started playing at a level we had never played before. With the momentum we built, we drove the game into overtime, and ultimately clinched the victory.

That turnaround felt exactly as Patanjali describes. It was like being in a "flow state," where we were going beyond our limits with ease. I felt it in my own performance as well. At one point, I managed to grab an offensive rebound away from the 7'1" center of our competitor, jump past him, and score—not just once but twice. At 5'10", I would have never thought I could do that.

To me, inspiration is like the soul's whisper flowing through the fibers of our existence. It feels like being connected to a force greater than ourselves, losing a sense of separateness, and surrendering control to that mystical force. This connection draws out our finest qualities in an effortless way, and that's not just in sports or the arts. It can happen while working in our jobs, responding to a disaster, or in an intimate conversation with a loved one.

This also applies to the totality of life. If we can find inspiration in life itself, the best in us will shine through in everything we do, across all the roles we play in life.

How inspiration comes into being is probably not fully within our control. Still, we can prepare ourselves to become a "magnet" for it. For some, that might mean seeking it through meditation, prayer, or even a walk in nature—practices that can lift us up, helping us feel centered and connected. Yet the question is, how can we draw it from the ordinary flow of life?

The approach we advocate in Soulgery rests on the premise that we are more likely to feel inspired when love and wisdom flourish within us. We can cultivate this by using our life experiences as opportunities to open our hearts to love and by purposefully gaining wisdom from them. We cover these two topics in chapters 5 and 6. Together, these practices elevate the level of consciousness at which we experience ourselves and life.

Along the way in this journey, we may feel the nudging of life's philosophical questions, especially about the meaning of our lives. A search for that answer can profoundly transform us, revealing that it can flow from within. It lifts us up from trying to be a magnet for inspiration to becoming a source of it.

SEARCHING FOR MEANING

A witty quote often attributed to Mark Twain highlights the unique significance of the search for meaning in life: "The two most important days in your life are the day you are born and the day you find out why."

Life's meaning is the answer we have to the question why we exist. The "why" question always has a special significance. Understanding the "what" or "how" of something gives us clarity, but deeply connecting with the "why" creates engagement, and drives us on a different level. The same applies to life as a whole. When we connect deeply with an answer to why we exist, our engagement and drive in the various roles we play become profoundly intense and meaningfully sustained.

Searching for meaning in life is like interpreting art—the art being the story of our lives. Some of history's greatest thinkers expressed their views on life's meaning with profound simplicity.[1] Pablo Picasso, Leo Tolstoy, and Ralph Waldo Emerson envisioned life's meaning as a blend of discovery and service to humanity:

- "Meaning of life is to find your gift, purpose of life is to give it away." —Pablo Picasso
- "The sole meaning of life is to serve humanity."—Leo Tolstoy
- "The purpose of life is not to be happy. It is to be useful, to be honorable, to be compassionate, to have it make some difference that you have lived, and lived well."—Ralph Waldo Emerson

For others, life's meaning is the pursuit of truth. This perspective resonates in the writings of the 19th-century American novelist and activist Eliza Farnham, and the Spanish philosopher and writer Miguel de Unamuno:

- "The ultimate aim of the human mind in all its efforts is to become acquainted with truth."—Eliza Farnham
- "My religion is to seek for truth in life and for life in truth, even knowing that I shall not find them while I live."—Miguel de Unamuno

[1] While these are widely attributed to their respective authors, their precise sources may not be entirely clear.

Then there are those, like Rumi, whose writings elevate love as the essence of life. His following quotes echo this conviction:

- "My religion is love. Every heart is my temple."
- "Love is the whole thing. We are only pieces."

While these are short quotations, if we had the opportunity to ask the authors why they concluded as they did, we would have caught a glimpse of their wisdom and philosophies and felt their love for life. The same goes for us as we search for the meaning of our lives. Whatever way we express it, whether in prose, poetry, or a picture, what gives rise to it has to be our wisdom, the love we hold in our hearts, and our philosophy of life.

A philosophy of life is a coherent story constructed out of our answers to the existential questions of life. While one can think of many of them, some, like these below, are especially relevant in the context of a search for meaning:

- What does it mean to be human? What differentiates us from the other species?
- How did we come to being? Is there a Creator, and if so, what is that Creator like? Is the Creator involved in our daily lives in any way?
- Is human life limited to the 70–80 or so years we exist on Earth, or is there such a thing as eternal life? If so, are there any connections between our eternal life and our life on earth?
- Is life predetermined or, are the outcomes in life a result of how we exercise our free will?
- Are there timeless principles which govern life?

Life's existential questions are eternal mysteries. They tend to pop up into our consciousness every now and then, especially during times of change. When they do, we may reflect on them for a while and then move on with our lives. Yet, these questions remain important, as they address the fundamental truths of our existence.

Ignoring them or putting them to the back burner of our minds is like playing a mystery game without any intention of solving it. A more proactive approach is to develop a personal philosophy, which involves continually broadening and deepening our thinking about life's existential questions, until we feel a deep sense of knowing the answers.

Our philosophical or religious inclinations may guide us in this journey. So can scientific discoveries. We will only feel that deep sense of knowing, however, once we experience the answers in our own lives, whether through a spiritual experience, in witnessing the power of our will, or recognizing a timeless principle which governs life.

The search for answers to life's existential questions can span a lifetime. Even if we hold strong beliefs, new experiences can prompt us to reevaluate them. Embracing this paradox— living by our beliefs while staying open to change—will take us further in this philosophical quest.

Becoming wiser and more openhearted will allow us to continually enrich and deepen our views on life's existential questions. At some point on this path, a sense of meaning can naturally emerge. Whether that meaning is to serve, seek truth, find love, grow, or something else, it becomes our inner source of guidance and inspiration. Connecting with that source in our daily lives puts us in a flow state more frequently than we will have experienced before, thereby awakening our greatest capabilities.

5

OPENING YOUR HEART

If you want the moon, do not hide from the night.
If you want a rose, do not run from the thorns.
If you want love, do not hide from yourself.
—Rumi

We seem to utter the word *love* more frequently than we experience it, using it to convey a range of positive emotions toward almost anything. Yet surely love transcends mere liking and is not just a temporary emotion?

Love has inspired humanity since the dawn of history. Artists have expressed it through countless forms, philosophers have debated its nature, and scientists have sought to explain it. Many regard love as an expression of the divine or of spiritual significance. However, despite centuries of contemplation and expression, love remains a mystery. What is it? How can one experience it?

While any answer to these elusive questions will be incomplete, the profound role love plays in the human experience compels us to explore its nature and impact. Love can be described as an enduring attraction, making us feel affectionate, joyful, compassionate, awe-struck, or left in a state of longing. It is an attraction which can bring out the best in us, prompting us to act without any expectations of reciprocity. It endures despite occasional feelings of frustration, jealousy, or anger toward the beloved.

We experience love beyond human relationships. We can feel it in our work, community, or nature. More importantly, we can love life and love ourselves. That gives us vibrancy, a sense of awe about the human experience, and enriches our interactions with the world around us.

While love isn't something we can control, it is probably safe to assume that we can influence whether we experience it or not. That invites an introspective approach to love rather than an outward pursuit, raising the question: how can we cultivate the right conditions within ourselves so that we can experience love?

A profound quote, which is often attributed to Rumi, can guide us in answering that question: "Your task is not to seek for love but to seek and find all the barriers within yourself you have built against it." Let's try to unpack this.

There are many barriers to love. If we are talking about romantic love between two people, there can be poor communication, constant criticism of one another, or an unwillingness to be vulnerable. However, if we are to look for a deeper, more fundamental barrier to love, our sense of self emerges as the prime suspect. A sense of self is integral to our humanity, defining our very identity. Yet, it can become a barrier to experiencing love in several ways.

Some of the thoughts we harbor about ourselves may act as a repellent to love. For instance, if we think of ourselves as unworthy, if feelings of guilt dominate our psyche, or conversely, if we see ourselves as inherently superior, experiencing love becomes a more distant prospect. When we become preoccupied—consciously or otherwise—with preserving or elevating our sense of self, we only reinforce that barrier. The thoughts and emotions springing out of this impulse can feel like a mass of clouds over our hearts, preventing love from finding its way in.

In this context, we can open our hearts to love only by recognizing and removing these inhibiting influences—whether they arise from limiting beliefs about ourselves or from an instinct to protect our sense of self. Although these influences are not always easy to notice, self-reflection allows us to spot the "footprints" they leave behind—subtle imprints in our thoughts, emotions, and behaviors.

These footprints can take many forms: feelings of jealousy, quickness to take offense, dependence on praise, or a tendency to feel victimized. They may also appear in subtler ways, such as favoring those who flatter us, avoiding inconvenient truths about ourselves, or becoming easily hurt. Even sarcasm, arrogance, or a lack of authenticity can often be traced back to the need to protect or elevate our sense of self.

Each time we notice one of these footprints and reflect on the role our sense of self has played, we create an opportunity to eliminate its inhibiting influence. While these moments of insight may feel insignificant, their cumulative effect clears the way for love to freely flow in.

Our more significant experiences can be ideal for such self-reflections. For me, a relatively recent example occurred during the early phases of working on *Soulgery*.

I decided to create *Soulgery* in order to make a positive difference in the lives of others in some way. As I went along, however, I discovered that I also had other motives, the first signs of which were the deep frustrations I felt in attempting to write it up. I was disliking passages which I had previously liked, reframing the story many times, doubting the value of what I was doing, questioning my abilities, you name it.

Reflecting on why it was such tough going, I spotted some typical reasons such as discovering fresh insights into the subject, and identifying new connections between the topics, all the while honing my writing skills. I also noticed something else: a desire for widespread recognition of my work was roaming through my mind all too much. This was diluting the focus I needed for producing high-quality content, causing me to waste time.

I finally admitted to myself that my motivation for Soulgery wasn't purely to make a difference in the lives of others. It was also to serve my sense of self. The irony wasn't lost on me that I was writing about the dangers of an impulse to serve one's sense of self but was unable to hold my own in check while doing so!

The impact of this self-discovery was profound. Recognizing that I had been influenced by a motive to serve my sense of self, I was able to let go of it. As a result, my focus naturally shifted to the work itself—creating meaningful content. More importantly, this shift allowed me to draw deeper insights from my experiences, and it inspired greater creativity in weaving them into Soulgery.

This taught me that, sometimes, awareness and acceptance are all we need; the rest follows almost effortlessly. Carl Rogers points to this contradiction in his 1961 book, *On Becoming a Person: A Therapist's View on Psychotherapy:* "The curious paradox is that when I accept myself just as I am, then I change."

Another lesson was the subtle and persistent nature of the impulse to serve the sense of self. I hadn't expected it to exert such a limiting influence while working on *Soulgery,* particularly because I believed I had already overcome this challenge before—during my departure from a prestigious executive position for reasons beyond my control.

As part of that exit, I was asked to address associates of the company in a town hall meeting right after the announcement. This gave me an opportunity to test whether I had allowed the prestige of that position to define who I was. I thought that if I could authentically do what a leader ought to do during an exit, I would be able to say to myself that I had kept my sense of self in check.

Fortunately, in this case I was able to address the audience in an authentic and effective manner, signaling that I had successfully contained the limiting influences of my sense of self. However, that test was merely about whether I was defining myself by virtue of my position. Passing it didn't mean that I would be able to keep my sense of self in check in other situations.

The inhibiting influences of our sense of self tend to show up in different contexts throughout our lives. Managing it in one context doesn't guarantee that we will be able to do so in another. The Soulgery example is only one of many. All of those experiences highlighted to me the need to remain vigilant about guarding my psyche for as long as I live.

Do these examples validate the premise that if we aren't serving our sense of self we are more open to love?

I can only speak for myself and say they do. *Soulgery* turned out to be a labor of love. Even though it took much longer than I initially envisaged, I felt increasingly attracted to it. Time flew by when I was working on *Soulgery.* I experienced a flow state many times. I feel grateful for all my experiences that led to the idea and for having had the time to develop it.

As for my exit from the executive role, the same holds true. I say this based on how I felt during my time with the company and how I feel about it now. My attraction to this company was always heartfelt. On numerous occasions, I have been told that when I spoke about my work and the company, my love for both was evident. My exit experience validated all of this.

Managing the influences of the sense of self can be a lifelong effort. Sometimes we may be unable to recognize its footprints in our experiences or connect them to our sense of self. The good and bad news is that the same signs will keep showing up on different occasions, providing more opportunities to recognize how we may be getting in our own way.

When we are able to spot those footprints, we have a chance to replace the impulse to serve it with a conscious decision to do the right thing. That frees up our mental and emotional energies to connect with life in more meaningful ways. These are the times when we truly open our hearts.

French mathematician, inventor, and philosopher Blaise Pascal wrote in his book *Pensées,*[1] "The heart has its reasons, which reason knows nothing of." This journey of opening ourselves to love is a quest of the heart, not of the mind. When we experience the mysterious and enduring attraction called love—whether toward an idea, a vision, or a person—our minds will understand what our hearts have known all along.

In the next chapter, we will discuss acquiring wisdom, another lifelong journey which is deeply interconnected with opening our hearts to love. Becoming wiser can deepen the love we hold in our hearts and, as we experience love, our understanding of ourselves and life expands.

---

[1] *Penseés* translates to "Thoughts" or "Reflections" in English.

6

HARVESTING WISDOM

Wisdom is not a product of schooling but of the lifelong attempt to acquire it.
—Albert Einstein

Wisdom is an enduring gift nestled within life's mysteries and complexities, waiting for those prepared to receive it. Its core is a deep understanding of how life truly works. The more closely this understanding aligns with reality, the wiser we become. This sharpens our judgment, refines our discernment of right and wrong, and deepens our love for life. Navigating life with wisdom is like traversing an uncharted landscape with a clear map in hand.

We are inherently limited in our ability to understand how life really works. We experience life within the constraints of our five senses and are bound by time and place. These and other limitations prevent us from explaining everything that happens around us. As John Lennon aptly put it: "Reality leaves a lot to the imagination." Consequently, each of us holds, as "our truth," a small and often semiaccurate sliver of what transpires in life. Harvesting wisdom is the lifelong journey of expanding that sliver, making it ever larger and more accurate.

How far we go in this journey is partly a function of our upbringing, education, and the human ecosystem in which we find ourselves. Yet, the extent to which we learn from our everyday experiences can be more influential than any of these factors. We can grow our wisdom at a compound rate when continuous learning is an integral part of our daily lives.

Our *ability to understand*—whether it's events or people—is fundamental to such learning. As basic as this ability seems, it is never perfect and can always be improved. All of us can enhance our understanding by practicing active listening, building questioning skills, and engaging in meaningful self-reflection.

Continuous learning has two other pillars. First is to maintain our humility, allowing us to keep the door to lifelong learning wide open at all times. Second is to cultivate our curiosity as a way of fueling our journey for as long as we live. We expand on all these pillars in the next three sections.

Ultimately, the essence of wisdom lies in understanding the cause-and-effect relationships in life. Said another way, wisdom grows from how we perceive the interplay of life's events. The insights we draw from our experiences continually shape this perspective. By connecting these insights in increasingly astute ways, we enhance the value of our wisdom. We delve deeper into how these connections come to life in the section titled "Unraveling Life's Causalities."

Wisdom is available to all, and life naturally imparts it to us. However, the key questions are: how much wisdom do we harvest, how fast do we acquire it, and how deeply do we reach? By developing an ability for continuous learning and persistently striving to paint an accurate picture of life's causalities, we truly push the envelope out in all of these dimensions.

A QUALITY UNDERSTANDING

In his 1973 book *The Human Province,* the Nobel Prize–winning writer and thinker Elias Canetti says, "Understanding, as we understand it, is misunderstanding." The quality of our understanding is rarely perfect. Numerous obstacles get in the way—being too absorbed in ourselves, a lack of care, or excessive multitasking, to name a few.

Some of these barriers are innately human. We cannot eliminate them, but we can minimize their distorting effects. Our emotions—discussed in more depth in chapter 14—are one such example. They can cloud our perceptions, obstructing our ability to truly understand. While we can't eliminate them, we can strive to manage their impact.

Our "self-lens" is another example. We perceive events from our own particular vantage point, shaped by our mindsets, passions, and biases. These factors distort our understanding in more ways than we often realize.

In one of my mentoring sessions, I was helping a mentee find a way to grow her business, which had reached a plateau. During our first few sessions, we explored different ways of tackling the problem but made no progress. A personal issue kept surfacing in our conversations, and I consistently set it aside, thinking it would be easy to resolve—because for me, it was. Only when I noticed how often this issue reappeared did I realize how difficult it was for her.

Once we addressed it, she was able to overcome that challenge. Interestingly, this cleared the way for her to solve the business-growth problem as well. My self-lens has led me to misjudge the significance of the personal issue, blinding me to the fact that solving it was the key to unlocking the business solution.

Another obstacle to a quality understanding is our propensity for action. There is often a tension between acting and understanding and we seem to err on the side of the former, especially if we are highly driven. Even those who are experienced and successful can fall into that trap. A developmental program I attended as an assessor brought that point home to me.

Participants in this program were fairly senior executives with aspirations for general management roles. Part of the program was a role-play exercise where the assessor assumed the role of the customer. The participant, as the supplier, was expected to reach an annual agreement with the customer within a specified time frame.

While the participants knew that a good agreement was only possible with a good understanding of the customer, many of them made their proposal too soon in the conversation. Had they taken more time for questioning to understand the customer better, they would have uncovered valuable insights. Their action orientation got in the way of a quality understanding and reaching better agreements.

These obstacles to a quality understanding will be with us for as long as we live. We can't remove our self-lens or survive without a level of action orientation. Yet, we can lessen their distorting effects by developing three core skills that improve the quality of our understanding: active listening, asking insightful questions, and constructing the right story about what we are seeking to understand.

Listening

Brenda Ueland, an American writer and teacher, described listening as a "creative force." In her 1941 article "Tell Me More" she wrote, "The friends that really listen to us are the ones we move toward." She highlighted the transformative power of active listening, stating: "When we are listened to, it creates us, making us unfold, and expand."

Active listening can unleash this creative force. It is listening with our whole selves—not just with our ears and minds, but also with our hearts and soul. It means tuning in not only to what is said but also to what is unsaid: the non-verbal cues like tone, gestures, and body language.

Listening is like tuning a radio in a storm—static and interference distract us, making it hard to catch the signal clearly. Our emotions, the tendency to form opinions too soon, or the urge to respond, are like background noise, pulling our attention away from the conversation. We often erect additional barriers, such as multitasking or failing to address distractions over which we have control. This is compounded by the barrage of noise in our digital era. At the heart of active listening is battling these distractions in real time. Techniques like asking clarifying questions or replaying what we heard can help us stay focused and engaged.

The saying "Practice is the best of all instructors"[1] applies most fittingly to developing basic skills such as listening. We can become better listeners by continually practicing active listening in our daily conversations, especially those we value most. The keys to this practice are preparation and reflection.

Preparing for active listening is about cultivating steadfast intentionality. In my experience, some of the best conversations I've had were those where understanding was my *only* goal—even when part of me was anxious to jump into action, or offer my perspective. Patience in those moments always proved worthwhile. When I listened actively, I often found breakthroughs in resolving issues, even when I wasn't focused on finding a solution. This kind of intentionality can arise naturally when we feel drawn to the topic or the person. When that's not the case, a conscious effort to cultivate genuine interest in the conversation becomes essential.

[1]By Pubililus Syrus, in his work *Sententiae*, specifically Maxim 439.

Reflecting on our important conversations can offer meaningful insights into how we listen. Taking a moment to consider what worked well and where we faced challenges can guide us toward stronger connections. Feedback from others can also shed light on areas to strengthen. With time and effort, these practices can transform the way we connect and communicate.

Active listening transforms us into listeners who naturally unleash the creative force that Brenda Ueland refers to, turning our conversations into opportunities for mutual growth and discovery.

Asking Questions

In life, we are more often rewarded for finding answers rather than coming up with insightful questions. This starts with schooling and continues throughout our adult life. We might even find ourselves in trouble if we ask too many questions. As a result, we grow stronger muscles for searching for answers rather than asking questions.

We can counteract this tendency through practice, just as we do when building listening skills. In this case, that means regularly flexing our questioning muscles in daily life—whether in pursuing our aspirations or tackling challenges.

This begins with giving ourselves the time to reflect on the questions that truly matter. A quote often attributed to Albert Einstein captures the significance of this: "If I had an hour to solve a problem and my life depended on it, I would use the first 55 minutes to determine the right questions to ask."

Even if Einstein's 55-out-of-60 approach may seem excessive, it is safe to assume that most of us err on the side of taking insufficient time to ponder incisive questions. So, what is the right amount of time? To answer, we can draw a parallel with building physical muscles. Just as strengthening real muscles requires discomfort, building our questioning muscles also means we step out of our comfort zones. Feeling that "burn" is a sign we are putting in the necessary effort.

Similar to developing active listening skills, we can fuel our progress by reflecting on how we inquire during a conversation. For instance, we can ask ourselves whether our questions served a clear purpose? Did they shift someone's perspective, lead to a solution, or show genuine care? Have they sparked debate or inspired engagement?

It's also valuable to consider the questions we didn't ask. With hindsight, we might identify inquiries that could have changed the flow of events. Additionally, the way we make others feel while seeking answers is a crucial measure of our skill. Even the most insightful questions can have unintended consequences, such as making others feel threatened, which diminishes their effectiveness.

Finally, and perhaps most importantly, recent advances in AI offer a unique opportunity to rapidly enhance our questioning skills. By engaging with AI as a "thinking partner," we can collaboratively explore real issues, testing and refining our approach. It's fascinating to observe how subtle shifts in phrasing can steer a discussion in different directions, ultimately leading to a deeper understanding.

Asking insightful questions helps us focus on what truly matters in what we are seeking to understand. Yet, this skill goes beyond understanding—it facilitates problem solving, leads to better decisions, and drives innovation. It can also be the creative force that Brenda Ueland refers to in the previous section. The seeds we plant with our questions can flourish into new ideas, discoveries, and change.

Thinking Big, Deep, and Long

In her poem, *The Speed of Darkness*, the American poet Muriel Rukeyser said, "The universe is made of stories, not atoms."

Understanding—whether it's events or people—involves constructing a story in our minds and hearts. Listening attentively and asking incisive questions reveal the fragments. The story emerges when we thoughtfully connect these fragments together, which often requires deep reflections. Here, we will propose an approach for that self-reflection that enriches our understanding—we call it, "big, deep, and long" thinking.

The *big* part is about striving to see the larger picture with its interrelated parts and its full context. We can understand anything in this way, even a single human being. The Self Map is an example of such holistic thinking. We can understand organizations, companies, nations, or any situation holistically. All of these operate in an external environment, where interactions between their parts and external influences shape their behavior as a whole.

Striving to recognize the bigger picture creates a healthy distance from what we are trying to understand, allowing us to overcome the distortions caused by our self-lens. It also surfaces new questions and insights. In a world where specialization dominates and analysis is far more emphasized than synthesis, adopting such a holistic view becomes increasingly valuable.

Big thinking allows us to see an overall picture. Yet, to understand the more precise cause-and-effect relationships, we may need to dig *deeper*, repeatedly asking why. This returns us to a childlike state, where our curiosity reignites and irreverent questions unlock hidden truths, revealing the root causes in most situations.

Finally, there is the time dimension—the *long* part—where we seek to understand the history of the story. Exploring its origins and evolution often reveals insights into the present and positions us better to project into the future. With big, deep, and long thinking, we view events in 3-D, construct stories that align more closely with reality and add greater depth and meaning to our experiences.

Understanding is like navigating through a complex landscape—it requires tuning in to all available channels for information, focusing on the important pieces, and reflecting on them to determine the best path forward. Since understanding is inherently imperfect, we can always expand our capacity for it. As we develop greater competence in the skills it requires, we gain the ability to quickly capture an accurate picture of our experiences, much like a camera that combines panoramic breadth with high resolution, bringing the full scene into sharp focus.

Leonardo da Vinci is widely credited with saying, "The noblest pleasure is the joy of understanding." To me, these joys include mastery, discovery, creativity, connection—and undoubtedly many more.

Let's now explore the other two pillars of continuous learning: humility and curiosity.

MAINTAINING OUR HUMILITY

In preparing myself for a senior leadership role, I decided to engage a coach. During our first session, the conversation took us to a discussion on humility. My coach said to me that humility in positions of higher authority can be risky. It may be perceived as a weakness and exploited, causing us to fall short in leadership qualities such as inspiring confidence.

I was disturbed by those comments because they went totally against one of my core values. As a response, I vigorously engaged her in a philosophical debate on humility, but that didn't go anywhere. In the end, neither of us changed our views, we agreed to disagree, and moved on.

When I think back on that exchange, I remember remaining cordial in the words I used, but not in my thoughts. More specifically, I was making judgments about my coach, assuming that she couldn't appreciate the depth of the concept of humility. I even concluded that her point of view was one of the root causes of the poor leadership we witness all the time.

I was so sure of my point of view, and so unwilling to listen to a different one, that I brought the conversation to a close. Those thoughts were a clear manifestation of the irony of arguing for the value of humility in an arrogant way, if not in words, certainly in thoughts.

Sometimes, even if we place a high value on a human quality like humility and attempt to honor it in our daily lives, it is easy to overlook those inescapable moments when we fall short in practicing it. Humility is tricky. It works best when paired with confidence; yet, paradoxically, confidence can sometimes hinder humility. We may consider ourselves outwardly humble but fail to recognize the deeper arrogance we project—just as I did with my coach.

Keeping our doors wide open for lifelong learning requires an unflinching belief that no matter how much we know, we still have a lot more to learn. No matter where we are in life, or what we might have accomplished, a part of what we know is likely to be wrong. One of my favorite quotes about lifelong learning is a Chinese proverb which says: "When the student is ready, the teacher appears." Humility is a commitment to being a student of life, actively learning from anyone, anything, at any time.

Even if we wholeheartedly agree with these beliefs, abiding by them is not always easy. The antagonist we met earlier—our sense of self—is determined to get in the way. In the story above, my arrogance and unwillingness to listen to my coach were clearly the footprints of an inhibiting sense of self. I just couldn't recognize them at that time. There might have been other footprints such as overconfidence or being closed to feedback. These were likely rooted in an unjustified sense of self-righteousness.

Had I kept a more open mind in that conversation, we might have explored some of the risks my coach mentioned, and I would have taken away useful insights. The fact that I remained unaware of this for years speaks to the difficulty of recognizing the inhibiting influences of our sense of self and underscores the importance of always remaining vigilant against its effects.

So what about the risks of embracing humility? I believe my coach was right: humility can be risky, especially in environments where assertiveness is valued more highly. It can sometimes be mistaken for uncertainty, making it harder to inspire confidence in those around us. We might find it difficult to promote ourselves, leaving others unaware of our contributions. Additionally, openness to feedback—a natural consequence of humility—can expose us to excessive criticism.

Yet, dismissing humility to avoid these risks is like using a sledgehammer to crack a nut—an unnecessary and disproportionate response that ultimately stifles our growth. Maintaining our humility doesn't preclude us from taking well-considered actions to mitigate these or other risks. The abundance of the fruits of lifelong learning far outweighs the risks.

CULTIVATING OUR CURIOSITY

The 19th century financier, statesman, and philanthropist Bernard Baruch is quoted as saying: "Millions saw the apple fall, but Newton asked why." Just like Newton, some people are naturally curious. My maternal grandfather was one of them. He retained his curiosity into the final days of his 106-year life.

His first 22 years were dominated by significant wars as he witnessed the waning days of the once vast Ottoman Empire. Most notably, he lived through the Balkan Wars, World War I, and the Turkish War of Independence. What I remember most about him though was his never-ending curiosity, which stayed with him until his last days.

In one of his visits to my house, I set him up to play chess against a computer program. He was 96 years old then, but still an avid player. After a pretty long game he unfortunately lost. He was in deep thought for a while after the game. Finally, he spoke, saying he couldn't understand which of his or his opponent's moves had caused him to lose.

My grandfather was both awed and humbled by the fact that someone could program a computer to beat a chess player with nearly 80 years of experience, without that player even realizing how he had lost. He then started asking questions about computers and how they play chess. We talked about hardware, software, algorithms, the speed of the computer, and even computer science education. He kept asking questions until he had settled in his own mind what had occurred.

On other occasions, he would ask me about topics which he knew I had an interest in. The depth and the breadth of his curiosity included religion, sports, philosophy, math, physics, history, politics, and more. Somehow, he was able to remain curious on a broad range of topics for as long as he lived. People like my grandfather naturally remain curious for life. The question is whether we can acquire this quality as well. We really don't know until we try.

Our curiosity will naturally get a bump as our lives change—like moving to a new location, taking on a new job, or entering a new relationship. A challenge we face can make us more curious. Advancing our skills in listening, asking questions, and thinking big, deep, and long can also fuel our curiosity. Yet, to remain curious for a lifetime, we may have to do more. Let's talk about two specific approaches.

The first is to make a conscious effort to connect with the joy of discovery. I. Claude Bernard[2] is often quoted as saying, "The joy of discovery is certainly the liveliest the mind of a human can ever feel." It is especially meaningful to hear this from such a consequential physiologist. Out of the many experiences of that joy, one I remember with a smile happened during my first year as a graduate student at Georgia State University in Atlanta.

One of the struggles I had back then was understanding newspaper articles, despite my extensive education in the English language. I started taking English lessons when I was 8 years old. All the math and science courses I took were in English. My entire university education—with the exception of a few courses—was in English. But I still couldn't understand the newspapers. So, I set a goal for myself to crack that nut as soon as I could and diligently worked on it.

---

[2] I. Claude Bernard was a 19th-century French physiologist who made significant contributions to the science of medicine. Bernard Cohen of Harvard University, author of books on the lives of Isaac Newton and Benjamin Franklin, called Claude Bernard, "one of the greatest of all men of science." The quote has been modified from "mind of a man," to "mind of a human."

Being able to understand an article about Valentine's Day was my first victory. What held me most in awe at that time was how an occasion like Valentine's Day could be used to create a sizable business. As boring as that may sound now, having gone to college in the 1970s, in a country with a much smaller economy, a different culture, and in a world which wasn't as globalized as it is now, that felt pretty new and energizing. This feeling of discovery lingered in my mind long after that experience, stirring my curiosity.

Each of us has likely felt similar joys of discovery many times. When our curiosity begins to fade, recalling those moments can reignite it—much like how remembering a first kiss rekindles a desire to feel that spark again.

The second approach is to integrate more *diversity* into our lives. Johannes Kepler, one of the prominent figures of the scientific revolution of the 17th century said: "The diversity of the phenomena of nature is so great and the treasures hidden in the heavens so rich, precisely in order that the human mind shall never be lacking in fresh enrichment."

Diversity is a gift from nature. It is everywhere: in the backgrounds of people, in cuisines, and in different forms of entertainment. There is great diversity to the types of urban landscapes we inhabit within a city, in media channels, in different political or religious beliefs, and so on.

Life offers more than enough diversity to keep us curious. Unfortunately, an inclination toward the familiar often holds us back from taking advantage of this. We can keep that tendency in check by consciously adding variety to our lives. When we find ourselves retreating to what's familiar, adding diversity—whether in people, places, cultures, or ways of thinking—can spark our curiosity anew.

Curiosity is the fuel for our lifelong journey in acquiring wisdom. One question to ask may be: can we have too much of it? Or to put it another way, can curiosity kill the cat? I guess the answer is: yes, it can. If we take curiosity to the extreme, we may perpetuate an addiction to learning with no clear purpose. That can cost us the focus required for what is really important. We will have to find the balance, on one side remaining curious, on the other, staying focused.

A journey of continuous learning founded on sharpening our skills, fueled by curiosity, and sustained by humility will keep us discovering countless lessons in the campus of life. Within this campus lies a capstone course, where we integrate everything we have learned to construct the bigger story of "life according to us." Let's now embark on that course.

UNRAVELING LIFE'S CAUSALITIES

We have already talked about cause-and-effect relationships as they relate to the quality of our understanding of people or events. The entirety of life is governed by a hypercomplex web of cause-and-effect relationships. From the microscopic level of our cells to macrophenomena like climate change or wars, there is a vast and intricate network of interactions which follow each other perpetually.

These causes and effects are both multidimensional and intertwined. They govern physical, intellectual, emotional, and spiritual realms for individuals, groups, humanity as a whole, and all forms of activity in our universe. We, as a species, have the boldness to attempt to unravel this hypercomplex web of cause-and-effect relationships of life. Our accomplishments over the course of our existence have been remarkable. We keep unraveling ever more insights into how life works.

We do the same as individuals. Based on our experiences, we shape our points of view on the cause-and-effect relationships of life. At any point in time, those views are more likely to be imperfect than perfect. Yet, life gives us the opportunity to constantly recalibrate our views. As Ralph Waldo Emerson captures a timeless truth in his 1841 essay Compensation: "Life is a perpetual instruction in cause-and-effect."

A pivotal challenge to receiving that instruction is to become a keen observer of cause-and-effect relationships. Often times, an intense desire for the effects we seek in life prevents us from being an acute observer of the causes.

Among the many places I have learned this was on the tennis court. I tried to pick up tennis without coaching in my early twenties. I didn't get to be a great tennis player, but a factor that improved my game was a realization that my desire to get the next point—the effect—often took focus away from mastering the proper technique to get that point—the cause. When I deliberately shifted my focus away from the score to doing the fundamentals correctly, I noticed that I not only scored better, I also identified other factors which made a difference to my game.

I experienced this principle in action in a different way during the early years of my general management career. Life's welcome kit to me at that time included a combination of natural disasters, political and economic crises, structural changes, and years of tailwinds suddenly turning into headwinds.

Delivering on our budgets during those years was tough. Yet, the external headwinds forced us to understand the drivers of results in a deeper and more granular way. This led us to allocate our limited resources efficiently. That wasn't enough to deliver on our budgets, but it helped us to perform better than our competitors. As importantly, it gave us a better understanding of the drivers of results, helping us build a stronger business for the years to come.

Maintaining the mental discipline to attentively observe life's cause-and-effect relationships enables us to draw wisdom from our everyday experiences. We reach a significant milestone in this journey when we begin to recognize causalities that extend beyond specific situations and apply universally. While life experience gradually reveals these connections, we can accelerate this process by cultivating two essential skills: associating and zooming out.

Associating

Cause-and-effect relationships that resonate universally are the invisible threads connecting seemingly unrelated events. Associating is the act of recognizing these threads.

For instance, I have learned that the rules of winning are the same in basketball—or any sport for that matter—as in business. If you have the right strategy, tactics, good execution, good teamwork, and belief, you are likely to win. But if winning makes you arrogant, you inevitably find yourself on a losing path. Only by learning from your losses and evolving can you return to winning.

It may sound surprising, but the causality of the luck factor operates similarly in life and in backgammon—a game I love to play. Luck in backgammon comes from the roll of the dice. Yet other factors, like tactics, experience, and agility, remain within our control. I'd even argue that managing one's psyche is also a crucial part of the game. When we allow the roll of the dice to inflate or deflate our self-perception, we miss opportunities to improve on those controllable factors.

In real life, luck manifests in different forms, but the causality is the same. When factors beyond our control influence our results and we mistakenly attribute those outcomes solely to ourselves, we overlook the chance to grow.

Each of us can draw similar associations from our own experiences, enriching our wisdom. These insights can simplify otherwise complex situations. One such example for me involves understanding what makes me most effective. I have learned that I perform best when working for a cause I believe in, alongside capable and trustworthy people, and within a structure that allows me the space to make a meaningful contribution. Recognizing this causality has streamlined my decisions about which initiatives to pursue.

Another way to identify broadly applicable cause-and-effect relationships is to zoom out—to view events from a higher vantage point.

Zooming Out

One of my earlier experiences with zooming out came during a functional leadership role. I realized that to truly excel, I needed to focus not only on fulfilling my role's responsibilities but also on strengthening cross-functional collaboration within the company. To do so, I had to step back and view the business from the perspectives of other function leaders and the CEO. This broader vantage point not only improved my performance, but it also taught me valuable lessons about causalities in business.

Zooming out is both a skill and a choice. Acquiring the skill or improving on it is the easier part. The harder part is making the choice to do so.

I recall a debate on how to improve gender diversity in corporate boards where the idea of establishing quotas was proposed. The arguments for and against the idea came from two distinct vantage points. The "for" side emphasized the need to recognize and correct historical biases. Meanwhile, the "against" side focused on a commercial perspective, arguing that forcing quotas would not lead to better decisions and businesses should be free to act in their own best interest. Ultimately, the "against" side won the day.

During the debate, neither side attempted to shift their vantage point. The "for" side made the case for the general benefits of diversity but was unable to frame their argument in a business context. Conversely, the "against" side remained fixated on a narrow view of shareholder value, limiting the role of a business in society to providing basic benefits, like jobs and taxes. They did not aspire to position the businesses as greater forces for good or consider how such an approach can sustainably grow shareholder value.

The participants in this debate were highly educated and experienced, clearly capable of elevating their vantage points. Most cared deeply about society and business. Nevertheless, they just didn't zoom out. This is a common dynamic in polarized discussions. The forces pulling us to entrenched positions can be powerful—whether vested interests, apathy, a sense of limited responsibility, or an unshakeable conviction in an idea. Sometimes, viewing issues from a broader perspective may not feel practical.

All of these reasons for resisting a shift in perspective can be valid. Yet, if we always yield to them, we remain confined to the same frame of reference. By occasionally stepping back to view events from an elevated position—even without immediate action—we can begin to uncover causalities that might otherwise remain hidden and enhance our effectiveness in our roles.

Unraveling the causalities of life means understanding the rules of this game called life. Each individual defines what winning the game looks like; but whatever it is, the better we become at identifying the right causalities, the greater our chance of success, and the more shrewd we become in playing our chosen game.

The Fine Art of Growing Wisdom

In his essay titled *Circles*, Ralph Waldo Emerson talks about how life and the human soul are always evolving, with each new experience contributing to a broader and more transcendent understanding of existence. He writes: "Because the soul is progressive, it never quite repeats itself, but in every act attempts the production of a new and fairer whole."

Harvesting wisdom is the continuous act of evolving a picture of reality in our hearts and minds. This picture takes form through observation, learning from others, and most importantly, from our lived experiences. Along this lifelong journey, with every act, "a new and fairer whole" emerges.

Wisdom is truly acquired when we begin to live by it. A story often attributed to Nasreddin Hodja, a popular scholar of the 13th century known for his satirical ways of imparting wisdom, makes that point in a simple and witty way.

> *One day a mother takes her son to Hodja, complaining that he eats too much sugar and requests Hodja's help. Hodja asks them to go home and come back in four months' time. When the mother and son return, Hodja tells the boy not to eat too much sugar and says nothing more. The mother gets upset and asks why they had to wait four months for such a simple answer. Hodja responds that before he could tell her son that he shouldn't eat so much sugar, he had to stop eating too much of it himself, and to do that he needed four months.*

Observing a certain truth about life or even agreeing with it doesn't mean that we have harvested any wisdom. Living by that truth does.

BACK TO "THE SOURCE"

Planet Earth is such a small part of the universe that it is less than insignificant. It probably can't even be seen from most parts of space. Every minute, it has about 200 new arrivals of individual human beings and about 100 departures. We are just one among the billions who pass through in a snippet of time.

That probably makes us feel insignificant, yet we yearn for significance, another human paradox. The truth in a paradox is revealed when we try to find a way for both sides of it to coexist, not by gravitating to one side.

How we can make the feelings of significance and insignificance coexist within ourselves can be a lifetime's work. Maybe there isn't a satisfactory answer. Clearly, simply accepting our insignificance won't do anything for us. But, trying to source inspiration from life by seeking the truth in it with an open heart can take us somewhere. If not to the final answer, it can bring us to the experience of higher levels of consciousness.

If that journey takes us to the meaning of our lives, we may find the answer there. A sense of meaning can make us feel the significance of our lives. Living out our lives to fulfill that meaning with humility may be the answer to the riddle of how significance and insignificance can coexist.

... ON TO ACT 2

In the last three chapters, we talked about an inward journey to cultivate our inner selves in a way which opens us to sourcing inspiration from life and to guide ourselves in a search for meaning. It is now time to shift our focus to the outside and talk about the impact we make in our various life roles.

Our wisdom, the love we hold in our hearts, and our skills flourish when we use them to make a difference in the lives of others. Acting in this way also requires a couple of inward journeys, which we discuss next.

ACT 2

AIM FOR IMPACT

7

YOUR IMPACT

A life is not important except in the impact it has on other lives.

—Jackie Robinson

The author of this chapter's quote made a significant impact on millions of lives. By breaking through the color barrier that once excluded African Americans from Major League Baseball, he inspired generations to combat racial prejudice both in and outside of sports. This quote is inscribed on Jackie Robinson's tombstone in Cypress Hill Cemetery in Brooklyn, symbolizing his perspective on what gives life meaning.

At first glance, his quote appears to advocate for an altruistic approach to life. The idea of making an impact on others is often seen as a hallmark of altruism, where one sets aside self-interest for the greater good. Yet, interpreting this quote through a binary lens of altruism-versus-selfishness misses a deeper insight: our own fulfillment in life is inextricably linked to the impact we make.

While some may intrinsically feel this connection, there are also tangible "returns" to be found in caring about the impact we make. Among the many forces that shape our lives—many of which lie beyond our control—our influence on others stands out as one we can consciously direct. More importantly, it plays a defining role in achieving what matters most to us. Whether advancing in our careers, nurturing families, or cultivating meaningful relationships, the impact we make on others remains central to these pursuits. Additionally, when we focus on our impact, growth follows naturally. It pushes us to see the bigger picture, think beyond immediate results, and, most importantly, deepen our understanding of others. With this perspective, we start noticing opportunities and risks we might have otherwise overlooked. Our goals become more meaningful, and the path to achieving them feels clearer and more intentional.

Even if we agree with all of this, it is still challenging to maintain focus on our impact to the extent it deserves. Inevitably, in our daily lives, more of our focus is on "what's in it for me" and that draws attention away from the impact we can make. Our impact deserves undivided attention from the moment we contemplate it to the moment we realize it.

This unfolds naturally when we instill an impact orientation deep within ourselves. We will explore two foundational concepts that underpin this orientation. The first is our source of motivation. When driven by a transactional mindset—focused on what we give and what we get—our impact tends to be limited. In contrast, by approaching life with a legacy mindset, our impact becomes more penetrating and lasting. Though the legacy mindset implies a longer-term outlook, it applies just as well to short-term actions. Embracing this mindset means always focusing on the difference we can make, whether we are at work, in a family role, or even in a single conversation. We expand on the legacy mindset and how we can internalize it in the next chapter.

We will then shift the discussion to the second concept that underpins an impact orientation: the "human qualities" which manifest themselves in our interactions. Human qualities are like fragrances. They cannot be seen but have an unmistakable presence. Just as certain fragrances can draw us in, certain human qualities connect us deeply and strongly with one another.

Words can be inadequate to convey the full meaning of a particular human quality. Traits such as integrity, care, humility, courage, tenacity, or respect can mean different things to different people. The effects of these qualities are nonetheless apparent. When others feel them in their interactions with us, we naturally amplify our impact. We expand on this in chapter 9.

By embracing a legacy mindset and embodying the qualities that unite us as human beings, we naturally create an enduring impact. This perspective leads us to the sweet spot between individuality and community, where achieving of our aspirations is accompanied by a deeper, more meaningful connection to the world around us.

Mahatma Gandhi is widely quoted as saying: "The best way to find yourself is to lose yourself in the service of others." In our quest to make a lasting and meaningful impact on others, we step beyond our comfort zones and uncover better versions of ourselves.

8

CREATING LEGACIES

What you leave behind is not what is engraved in stone monuments but what is woven into the lives of others.

— Pericles of Athens

A legacy is often understood as a grand accomplishment which echoes through generations. Yet, it can also be interpreted in a more personal and intimate context. Taking inspiration from this chapter's quote by Pericles, we can think of a legacy as something we create that touches the lives of others in a meaningful way. This broader definition of a legacy encompasses nearly everything we do in our life roles. At work, we create products, services, experiences, policies, or cultures. In our family lives, we nurture relationships, improve the skills of our children, or shape their characters. When these everyday creations weave into the lives of others and endure, they become our legacies. Enriching the concept of a legacy in this way allows us to recognize how seemingly small actions can leave a lasting imprint on the lives of others.

Often, what we do in our daily lives feels ordinary or inconspicuous. However, that doesn't mean these actions lack significance. A striking example of this for me is how a verse in a poem by the 19th century Ottoman-Turkish poet, Tevfik Fikret, transformed my life.

Fikret was the voice of freedom in his time. His poems sometimes had a rebellious tone, rejecting anything that put shackles on individual freedom. He didn't have the easiest time with the Ottoman government, but he kept writing about what he believed in. Fikret had a profound influence on Mustafa Kemal Atatürk, the founder of modern Türkiye. Atatürk once credited him with igniting the spirit of the Turkish Revolution that he led, transforming the Turkish people from subjects of the sultan into equal citizens of a nation-state.

Atatürk passed that spirit on to the teachers of the nation in a speech he gave in 1924, when the Turkish Republic was just one year old. In this speech, he challenged the teachers to raise generations who are free in thought, conscience, and wisdom. When I first heard those words, it took me a while to fully understand what he had meant. Freedom of thought was easy enough to grasp. I saw freedom of conscience as following one's inner sense of morality in discerning the right from wrong, rather than relying on dogmas.

Comprehending the phrase "freedom of wisdom" was more difficult. I had to refer to an Ottoman language dictionary to better understand the word, which I translated into English as wisdom. The original word was *irfan*, which means a deep understanding or sensing that takes one to the truth. Based on that, I reckoned that freedom of *irfan* means that we should be free to seek the truth about life and about ourselves in any way we like. Those words Atatürk used in his speech were the same words Tevfik Fikret used in one of his poems where he said:

I expect no gifts from any, nor beg for any wings
On my own I soar, in my own sky, in my own heavens
To bow is a heavier burden than a yoke
I am a poet who is free in thought, conscience, and wisdom.

Fikret published this poem in 1911 in a book titled *Haluk's Notebook*. Haluk was Fikret's son. Fikret passed away in 1915, but nine years later his verse found life in Atatürk's vision for the education system of Türkiye, paving the way for generations to be raised with freedom of thought, conscience, and wisdom.

While the execution of this vision has been far from perfect, its pursuit made a significant difference in all walks of life in Türkiye. Personally, I don't think I would have come close to doing what I have done in my life if I didn't feel free to have my own thoughts, to take my own conscience as a guide, and to build my own wisdom about myself and about life.

It took me a long while to appreciate how Fikret's legacy was woven into my life in such a transformational way. I don't know how many people in Türkiye would give him credit for the freedoms they enjoy today, even after reading this. Likewise, Fikret, surely wouldn't have known that his legacy, which he must have intended mainly for his son's benefit, would make the most profound impact on generations to come in Türkiye.

Our own legacies are similar. We cannot fully grasp their significance, the ripple effects they generate, or how others will build upon them. Much of this will develop beyond our control. Yet, when we approach our daily lives with a legacy mindset, we increase the likelihood that our impact is meaningful and lasting. This means recognizing that everything we do weaves into the lives of others—and choosing to act in ways that leave a lasting imprint. It also means embracing a broad perspective on our contribution. It can emerge from what we build over years and decades or from the thoughts and emotions we inspire in everyday moments.

The seed of this mindset is a strong intrinsic drive to make a difference for others. While this may come naturally to some people, it can also be cultivated. As we laid out in the previous chapter, constantly asking "What's in it for me?" weakens the intensity of this desire. Instead, recognizing the inextricable links between our impact, success, and fulfillment strengthens it.

The legacy mindset takes root as we engage in creations that touch others' lives in meaningful ways. With each experience, it grows stronger, reinforcing itself through the impact we see and feel. Over time, as these moments accumulate and shape our perspective, the mindset becomes second nature, guiding how we approach our various roles in life.

Let's now explore the core of this process: creation. As the saying goes, everything is created twice: first within us, and then in the real world. The first creation is a vision, an aspirational picture we paint in our hearts and minds. That vision is then brought to life through planning and acting on that plan with perseverance. Creating legacies is no different—whether their impact is immediate or takes years to unfold.

THE FIRST CREATION: ENVISIONING

A vision is a vivid image of an aspirational future we believe we can create, which drives us intensely toward its realization. It isn't merely a wish but something we see clearly in our hearts and minds. It is time-bound, and its expression allows us to determine whether we have attained it when that time comes.

Coming up with a vision can be like a tug-of-war between our imagination and intellect, between the best picture we can dream up and the reality of the world we live in. The art is to land as close to our imagination as we can, to conceive an aspirational vision which we can bring to life. As Michelangelo, the renowned Renaissance master, is often quoted as saying: "The greater danger for most of us lies not in setting our aim too high and falling short, but in setting our aim too low and achieving our mark."

This quote may feel contrary to one's concept of accountability. In certain contexts, not meeting expectations can have serious consequences. Yet, for our legacies, the greater danger is indeed to set the bar too low. That is simply because a vision is also a decision—one that determines not only the significance of the impact we aim to make but also how far we are willing to go to discover our better selves. In that tug-of-war between our imagination and intellect, leaning toward our imagination will take us farther, as long as we aren't totally detached from reality.

Some people are natural visionaries. During a dinner conversation with a colleague, I had a chance to hear the inspiring story of her father, who transformed a small mom-and-pop retail business in a medium-sized city in Türkiye, into a multinational technology company. This company now has operations in over 30 countries, from Asia Pacific to North America, with big global names as clients. Over the past 70 years this business reinvented itself a number of times.

When I hear a story like this, I can't help but wonder what drives people like my colleague's father. An anecdote gave me a part of the answer. She once told me he didn't like looking at photo albums because he felt that time was better spent thinking about the future. It struck me how strongly he favors imagining over reminiscing.

While this may come naturally to some, envisioning is a uniquely human ability all of us possess—one that can be refined through practice. It calls for a state of mind that sets aside everyday pressures, along with the thoughts and feelings that weigh us down. Sometimes we naturally slip into that imaginative state. It might happen when starting a new job, moving to a new location, beginning a new relationship, becoming a parent, retiring, or just wandering off into the future for no obvious reason. When we find ourselves in such a mood, seizing the moment may be all we need.

At other times, that state of mind may seem distant. We may feel as though we are running on a treadmill with no end in sight, unable to step off. Perhaps, bad experiences have chipped away at our hopes to a point where reigniting them feels impossible. These moments serve as silent drumbeats, urging us to shift our perspective.

A quote from John Berger, the influential art critic and author of *Ways of Seeing,* offers inspiration for responding to these drumbeats: "All creation is in the art of seeing."

We can see our lives in a refreshing way by adopting a panoramic view and a long-term horizon. A panoramic view means redirecting our focus from ourselves to the key stakeholders in our lives—spouses, children, colleagues—and considering life from their vantage points. This shift in perspective can inspire ideas about how we might make a meaningful difference in their lives. By expanding our perspective through a long-term lens, we reframe our thinking and open ourselves to imagining possibilities, as if beginning with a blank canvas.

This approach also positions us for more significant accomplishments. In tech circles, it's often said that people tend to overestimate what they can achieve in the short term and underestimate what they can achieve in the long term. The same holds true for us as individuals. When we set aspirations with a longer time horizon and make consistent progress, we not only accomplish more but also create meaningful legacies.

The length of that time horizon depends on what we are trying to achieve. For example, if we are creating a product, a service, or a new organization, that may take years. If we are setting out to transform agriculture around the world, to achieve sustainability and efficiency, it may need decades. A relationship may take a number of years to reach a certain milestone, or even a lifetime. Inculcating certain skills in our child could take months. Creating lasting impressions on others with our words and actions might be achieved within a single day, or in the flash of an eye. Whatever the time frame—years, months, or minutes—envisioning our legacy is a powerful step toward realizing it.

The first creation is only complete when we feel passionate about our vision and confident that we can realize it. Sometimes, we have to consciously build belief in ourselves and in those our vision touches, whether our children, partners, friends, parents, or colleagues. This usually involves another tug-of-war, this one between doubting and believing.

One of my leadership roles gave me an opportunity to build a new organization. When I learned that a well-respected colleague was available, I reached out to him to gauge his interest for an important role. I was thrilled to learn that he felt quite upbeat about the opportunity to work in our new organization.

Shortly after we started to work together, trouble started brewing. I realized that the culture of doing business in the new organization was different to the one in which my colleague had previously thrived. That caused him to struggle in his new role, and he wasn't performing up to my expectations. As my attempts to improve the situation kept failing, I began feeling discouraged.

While part of me was thinking that maybe this wasn't going to work out, another part of me trusted my initial instincts, believing in my colleague's good intentions, talent, and capacity for change. I decided to do something to activate him for that change. We had reached such a point that I felt I had to be very clear about what needed to happen, and if that didn't happen, we would have to part ways. I wanted to do that in a way that would enhance the chances of a turnaround. My idea was to share with him my feeling that the chance of a turnaround was small but not zero; yet, we owed it to ourselves to try.

The conversation wasn't an easy one, but it worked. As he changed, he began to collaborate effectively, and the quality of his work improved significantly. My vision for the organization was realized, and his career continued on a great path long afterward.

We can at times succumb to the doubts we have about others, or about ourselves, too soon. Yet, if we allow ourselves time to come up with ideas about how to eliminate our doubts and act on those ideas, we can strengthen our convictions. Going the extra mile in that tug-of-war between doubting and believing can pave the way for inspiring turnarounds.

Each of us has the ability to conceive aspirational visions of a better future, a skill we can continually improve with practice. This involves dedicating time for self-reflection, drawing both from our imagination and intellect, and sharing our dreams with others. Often, pieces of a vision brew in our minds for a period of time, eventually coalescing into a vivid picture we feel passionate about and believe in.

Reaching this point means we are already more than halfway toward realizing our aspirations. That said, it is important to recognize that executing our vision—the second creation—is just as crucial.

THE SECOND CREATION: BRINGING IT TO LIFE

A statement often attributed to Pablo Picasso is: "Our goals can only be reached through a vehicle of a plan in which we must fervently believe, and upon which we must vigorously act. There is no other route to success."

The same holds true for realizing the visions we have for our legacies. We first have to develop a plan to bring them to life. Depending on the legacy we have in mind, that plan can range from a set of mental notes to an elaborate list of interconnected tasks to complete, deadlines to meet, and resources to acquire. Whatever the plan, the key is to think pragmatically about how we will bring our visions to life, with focus on a few questions:

- What goals should we set which, if accomplished, will help us reach our vision?
- What is the right set of actions to take, their timing, and sequence?
- What resources do we need?

We delve deeper into planning in chapter 11. While that discussion focuses on a personal context, the concepts explored are equally applicable to planning our legacies. Given the wealth of resources available on this topic, we will not elaborate further here, except to highlight one key point.

No matter how simple or complex a plan may be, aside from the factors beyond our control, its fate hinges on the human factor: are the people impacted by our vision motivated by it; will they play their part; will they persevere? Harnessing the power of the human factor is critical to creating any legacy—be it a new enterprise, a relationship, skills, or the character of our children. That requires us to be relentless in striving to bring out the best in others. The discussion in the next chapter is especially relevant to this.

A LABOR OF LOVE AND A PATH TO LOVE

Austrian poet Rainer Maria Rilke likens creation to a birth. Like birth, there is intense labor in creating legacies. We have already discussed much of that labor. The obstacles we face along the way will only intensify this process.

Our love for life, or for those we hope to impact with our legacies carries us through this labor, revealing the joys of creation in the process: dreaming, sharing the creative experience, and witnessing the differences we make in the lives of others.

Conversely, creation is also a path toward love. Rumi is often quoted as saying: "Lovely days don't come to you; you should walk to them." Creating legacies is one of those walks. On this path, we are likely to meet a familiar antagonist—our sense of self—just as I did while writing *Soulgery.* It is in our nature that a desire to serve our sense of self often accompanies our aspiration to make a difference in others' lives. Keeping that motive in check, ensuring it doesn't overshadow our genuine desire to make a difference, is a crucial stepping stone in our walk toward love.

The impact of our legacies may exceed our expectations or fall short of them. Surpassing our expectations can test our humility, while falling short can challenge our perseverance. Yet, a hallmark of this path of love is to keep walking, undeterred by neither success nor by failure, until the legacy mindset becomes second nature.

9

ACTING HUMANLY

Good character is not formed in a week or a month. It is created little by little, day by day. Protracted and patient effort is needed to develop good character.

—Heraclitus

On one of my trips to Ankara, Türkiye, my mother shared a story she had found inside the sleeve of a classical music CD entitled *Kempff Plays Beethoven.* It was about Jean Sibelius, a Finnish composer widely regarded as his country's greatest, and Wilhelm Kempff, the legendary German pianist and composer. Sibelius is often credited with helping Finland develop a national identity during its struggle for independence from Russia. Kempff, meanwhile, is considered one of the greatest pianists of all time.

Recognized for his talent at just nine years old by the professors of the Berlin Musikhochshule, Kempff was particularly noted for his ability to transpose complex pieces from memory. Over the course of a remarkable career, he gained international acclaim for his lucid interpretations of composers like Mozart and Beethoven. His performances of Beethoven, in particular, were said to bring audiences closer to the legendary composer's spirit, as if he were channeling Beethoven's passion.

In later life, he settled in Positano, Italy where he taught exceptionally talented pianists. He assumed the role of a pedagogue, helping his students to mature as individual personalities, rather than making them imitators of his own style.

In May 1957, Kempff paid a visit to Sibelius, who, at the time, had only a few months to live. According to Kempff's account in his book *Was ich horte, was ich sah* (What I heard, what I saw), Sibelius asked him to play Beethoven's Hammerklavier Sonata, a piece Kempff had performed during the last time they were together. Kempff, deeply moved by the experience, describes it as follows:

> *The man's gift of summoning up all his spiritual forces, even when listening, reaches across to me. It is as if I am a runner in the Olympic relay. I take the flame from him and carry it onwards. It is during the Adagio, the most magnificent monologue Beethoven ever wrote, that it fully dawned on me that this is the only work which may fittingly be played for him, the great lonely man of Järvenpää, at this hour. When I have finished, he says to me, you did not play like a pianist, you played like a human being.*

"Playing like a human being" beautifully crowns the human qualities manifested in this story. The *care* these gentlemen had for music and for each other awakened the spiritual forces which captivated them both. Kempff's realization of how fitting it would be to play the Adagio from Beethoven's Hammerklavier Sonata to his friend is another example of his deep *care* and *respect* for Sibelius. For me, Kempff assuming the role of a pedagogue to assist his students mature as individual personalities, rather than creating replicas of himself, is an expression of the *respect* he had for their individuality.

These human qualities connected the two gentlemen as if in a torch relay. They built on each other's intellect, emotion, and spirituality. Kempff's ability to connect audiences with the revered composer's passion, even a century after his passing, speaks to the mystical power of the human qualities he embodied.

Playing like a human being can also serve as a fitting metaphor for how we act as professionals, parents, or partners. The human qualities that connect us can create equally moving experiences as we engage with each other, paving the way for a meaningful and lasting impact. The question is: what are those human qualities, and how do we make them our own?

Since a particular human quality can mean different things to different people, the answer to the first part of that question is deeply personal. Each of us must determine which qualities resonate most, understand their impact, and decide why they matter. To facilitate this self-reflection, in the following sections, I will share my own deliberations on two human qualities—fairness and integrity. My aim is not to prescribe a way of viewing these traits but to foster a deeper exploration of the human qualities we value.

As for the second part of the question—how to make these qualities our own—Aristotle provides timeless guidance in his seminal work, *The Nicomachean Ethics*: "The moral virtues, then, are produced in us neither by nature nor against nature. Nature, indeed, prepares in us the ground for their reception, but their complete formation is a product of habit." We can, indeed, make a human quality an integral part of our character by consistently acting in line with it. Yet, life will inevitably present us with trade-offs that make it difficult to do so. We will explore how to navigate these trade-offs after the discussions on fairness and integrity.

FAIRNESS

My paternal grandfather had a distinguished career as a judge during the period of the Ottoman Empire—early 1900s—and in the Republic of Türkiye after 1923. At the end of his career, he served as the president of the Supreme Court of Türkiye. Unfortunately, he passed away before I was born, but I gained precious insight into the concept of justice from reading one of his speeches. It was given to mark the opening of the judicial year of 1951–52. Addressing the judges in attendance, he said:

> *The progress of civilization and raising the level of our nation depends on the hard work by free will, of every member of the society, free of any fear, and confident of protection of their rights. This is possible only when the scales of justice are in perfect balance. The eyes watching these scales are so sensitive that even*

> *the slightest favoring of either side, even those deemed unimportant by you, will reflect in people's hearts as fear of injustice.*
>
> *This fear is a barrier to the progress of our nation. Those nations whose judges can defy their rulers with confidence will take their place among the select leaders of civilization. The judges who create such feelings of trust and confidence in the hearts of their people hold the prime place in preparing for such leadership. Your most important reward in this arduous work is the Nation's trust in you. Your most important service is to strengthen that trust.*

Although my grandfather's speech was about justice at a macro level, the points he made resonated with me at a personal level when I considered the human quality of fairness. The feeling of justice indeed penetrates us to the depths of our hearts and, just as how the fear of injustice halts the progress of nations, seeds of injustice we sow in people's hearts come back to us in potentially disruptive ways. Gauging fairness by the feelings we evoke in the hearts of others set a very high standard for me.

I recognize that I can't respond to every feeling of injustice, as some of them would be ill-founded. Likewise, I shouldn't extend that kind of sensitivity to everyone. Yet, in the right context, I can understand that living up to such a high standard connects us strongly and meaningfully with one another.

As to why judging our fairness by the feelings we evoke in the hearts of others is important, I found the answer in my grandfather's comment: "Your most important reward in this arduous work is the Nation's trust in you." Trust is a hard-earned, easily broken, and undervalued treasure. Such a high standard for fairness is the best way to preserve it.

INTEGRITY

The concept of integrity often arises in business meetings where companies discuss the values guiding their decisions. It was after one such meeting that I clarified what integrity meant to me.

One of the participants at this meeting proposed a definition of integrity: doing the "right" thing. The group quickly embraced this definition, but the ensuing discussion was more complicated. The first point of contention was around "Doing the right thing for whom?" Is it the right thing for the employees, the boss, the department, the shareholders, other stakeholders of the company, the economy, society, or humanity? Then there was the question of when? Is it the right thing for now, for this month, quarter, year, the next 10 years, or forever?

Discussion around those questions made it clear that the right thing for a business can differ depending on the bigger picture and time frames one considers. The group ended up embracing a concept of the right thing for all of the stakeholders of the company with a long-term view. That helped them find clarity on what integrity meant as they went about their business.

On reflection, defining integrity as an unwavering commitment to doing the right thing resonated deeply with me. However, what is right or wrong can sometimes be so nebulous that whether we consider it through a nuanced moral lens or through a binary good-or-bad one, defining it can be a real challenge.

The moral lens can invoke different value sets, religious beliefs, philosophies, or traditions. Each can have different answers about what is morally right. To make it even more elusive, as we and our societies change, our views on what is morally right or wrong can also change.

A light-hearted and amusing, but slightly worrying, story is the way people's feelings toward J.R. Ewing—a character from the TV series *Dallas*—have changed since the late 1970s. TV was introduced into Türkiye in the late 1960s. Since then, a number of U.S. TV series have captivated audiences. Among them was *Dallas*, whose popularity meant that one of its main villains, J.R. Ewing, played by Larry Hagman, quickly became a hated figure in Türkiye!

During the 1970s, there was no question in people's minds that the character's behavior was unethical and evil. Forty years on, when the show is run again, some of my friends said they didn't feel the same way as previously. They thought he was just a tough businessperson. I have to admit, I agreed with my friends!

The good or bad lens doesn't always provide a clear perspective, either. I can argue that it is impossible to know what is good or bad. For one thing, there is always good in bad and bad in good. Also, good or bad are the judgments we make based on how we look at events at the time we look at them. How scenarios unfold, and how we think about them at a future point in time is unknowable.

While defining the right thing can be an elusive task, the principles honored in that business meeting can be as helpful to us as individuals as they were to that company. Thinking with a perspective beyond ourselves, over a long-term horizon, and with a heightened sensitivity for fairness can guide us in determining the right moves.

As for why integrity is important, fostering trust is an obvious answer. I also realized that integrity gives us a power of legitimacy. Once others feel that we are inclined to do the right thing, we naturally garner support from others, positioning us to make a greater impact.

WHERE IT MATTERS

It is easy to act with the right human qualities when we have nothing to lose. What really matters is that we act with them even when there are trade-offs, whether real or perceived.

Among many such trade-offs, I recall one happening when we were acquiring a business which wasn't doing too well. The negotiations took a few months. In the final phase, the teams reached a point of agreement on everything except the price. The seller's team decided to take the issue to their owner.

I had met this owner just once, a year or so before the start of the negotiations. It was a memorable encounter. I visited him in his summer house to introduce myself and to talk about the business. He greeted me with a bear hug, which felt genuine. We spent hours talking about a wide range of topics and parted with mutual feelings of warmth.

As his team briefed him on the deal, he told them to tell me that I was to decide on the final price by myself. The gap we faced was an important amount for my company. I thought it was important to him as well. You might call this move a savvy one on his part, and it might have been. But when I place his decision in the context of our earlier encounter, for me, it was a genuine show of trust. I decided to reciprocate that by being fair, splitting the difference with him. I later heard that this decision was very well received by all.

At the time of making this decision there was a clear trade-off between living the human quality of fairness and achieving the financial results of my company. Yet, in my view, that was more perceived than real. The support of the seller in the implementation phase of an acquisition is generally critical to unlocking the full potential of the business being acquired. It was no different in this case. My decision helped create a more collaborative environment for the implementation phase. That most likely unlocked more value than the financial effect of splitting the difference with the seller.

However, at the time of making that decision, there were no guarantees that working collaboratively would generate incremental value. Measuring this value—even today—would be nearly impossible, as we'll never know what would have happened with less collaboration. The uncertainty and subjectivity involved in these kinds of decisions can easily make us feel that there is a trade-off to be made in living the right human qualities. This perception is probably not unique to the issues we face in our work roles.

Sometimes, the trade-offs can be real. Holding true to our convictions can make us unpopular, or worse. Going back to my grandfather's speech for example, defying the will of powerful rulers can come at a high personal cost. Those are the tougher decisions in our lives. Often, there are plenty of gray areas and, frequently, the case can be made for not being too idealistic. Yet, approaching these decisions with a pure intent to do the right thing will give us a solid platform from which to make those trade-offs.

Managing Our Intensity

Our intensity can be a subtle yet formidable barrier to embodying the human qualities we hold dear. Being productive, focused, or creative requires a certain level of intensity. When that intensity is exclusively dedicated to the task at hand, it can overshadow the human qualities which connect us with one another.

In our various roles, what predominantly defines our relationships are responsibilities and expectations. When responsibilities aren't fulfilled or expectations go unmet, conflicts arise. These conflicts can sometimes frustrate us to a point where we violate the unspoken rules of human interaction—such as making a disrespectful or uncaring comment—which can leave a lasting impact on others.

All of us experience this. A way to guard ourselves against it is to recognize that there is more to our relationships than the roles we play. Whether as coworkers, spouses, or citizens, we engage with each other first as human beings, then through those roles. Acting intensely and humanly aren't mutually exclusive. In fact, they are complementary. When we can activate both, we perform better. Acting humanly can enhance our performances at least as much as an intense focus on the tasks at hand.

RISKS AND REWARDS

Human qualities connect us deeply and strongly with one another, yet extending them to others is not without its challenges. When our good intent is misinterpreted or even used against us, we may face bitter lessons. Still, it is better to embrace these human qualities and learn how to extend them with discernment rather than dismiss them altogether. This is because they resonate with more people than we might expect, bringing out similar qualities in them and unleashing our collective genius.

As an international business executive, I was often asked how I handled cultural differences. While I recognized their relevance, I always believed that our shared humanity mattered far more. These intrinsic traits transcend cultural divides, social status, age, and gender, making them universally effective. Teams connected through human qualities not only performed well, their members usually displayed a deeper sense of fulfillment.

The 13th century Sufi mystic Haji Bektash Veli beautifully captured the essence of humanity when he said, "The human is hidden in the invisible." Our true nature indeed lies beneath the surface, defined by traits that may not be immediately visible. Embodying those that strongly connect us with one another leaves lasting impressions in our everyday interactions and amplifies the impact of our legacies. Most importantly, they make us more human.

... ON TO ACT 3

The second Act of Growth we have just discussed centered on the impact we make through our legacies and the human qualities we consistently demonstrate. Our ultimate aim was to instill an impact orientation within ourselves, naturally driving us to make a meaningful difference. Now, we turn our attention to bringing this orientation to life in a distinctive way: performing with excellence in our various roles.

• ACT 3 •

PERFORM WITH EXCELLENCE

10

YOUR RHYTHM

Life's like a play; it's not the length, but the excellence of the acting that matters.

—Seneca, *Epistulae Morales ad Lucilium*[1]

We are performing artists. We take part in this play that is life as professionals, parents, partners, or friends. Everything we do is a performance: the conversations we have, the presentations we make, our conduct in the meetings we attend, and even the messages we write. Excellence in those performances can change minds, touch hearts, and alter the course of events for the better.

Excellence is an elusive concept. We judge it according to our expectations, previous performances, or knowledge of the matter at hand. It is never static. What is considered excellent today may be viewed as merely satisfactory—or even mediocre—in the future. Nonetheless, excellence can be an actionable concept if we think of it as a journey—one where we continually strive to surpass our previous best, setting high expectations for ourselves, and upon meeting them, raising them to the next level.

Discipline forms the foundation of this journey, grounding us with focus and precision. Yet, even more essential is discovering the *rhythm* that works

[1]English translation: *Moral Letters to Lucilius.*

uniquely for us. Without this unique rhythm, you are like the pianist who hits every note perfectly but doesn't flow with the music.

For instance, in our professional lives, discipline helps us stay focused, meet deadlines, and maintain consistency. When applied too rigidly, however, it can stifle creativity, holding back breakthrough results. Likewise, at home, discipline can establish a helpful routine, but too much structure can leave little room for spontaneity, leading us to miss valuable opportunities to forge deeper emotional connections.

The challenge is to maintain a level of discipline that allows space for finding a rhythm that leads to true performance excellence. To explore this, we will borrow a concept from the business world—*performance management*—and adapt it for our purposes.

Businesses drive their performance through careful planning, resource management, focusing on execution, and investing in capabilities. These core principles can be applied just as well to our individual lives to help us find a rhythm which leads to performance excellence. We will discuss them in the next four chapters as follows:

1. Chapter 11: "Planning for Excellence"—Positioning ourselves for a better future
2. Chapter 12: "Managing Time"—Making the best use of the most precious resource we have
3. Chapter 13: "Performing for Impact"—Preparing for our performances and learning from them
4. Chapter 14: "Investing in Core"—Nurturing our well-being physically, emotionally, intellectually, and spiritually

As the performing artists of life, we face unique challenges on this journey. No one defines for us the work involved in being a parent, a partner, or a citizen. We figure it out as we go along. Nor do we get any formal training for the skills required for these roles. Our roles as professionals may be somewhat better defined, with job descriptions to guide us, but even then, gray areas abound. In addition, we must perform on demand, juggling multiple roles, while navigating uncertainties every day.

Against the backdrop of these challenges, the next four chapters offer a perspective for discovering our unique rhythm to perform with excellence. By experimenting with these ideas and evolving our approach, we create the conditions for this rhythm to settle in. As it does, performance excellence will naturally follow.

11

PLANNING FOR EXCELLENCE

Plans are nothing; planning is everything.

—Dwight D. Eisenhower, speech to the National Defense Executive Conference, November 14, 1957

There is a Turkish proverb which says, "While we make our plans, our fate laughs at us." It is true that no matter how good a planner one may be, most plans become outdated before we bring them to fruition—often sooner than we expect. Yet, the value of planning, especially personal planning, lies in the process rather than the output.

Personal planning is like taking a timeout in a sports game, allowing us to reground in reality and then reposition—both rationally and emotionally—for a better performance. It is an exercise in self-reflection, not to overthink but simply to check in with ourselves. Clinical psychologist Paul T.P. Wong, known for his work on meaning-centered therapy, describes self-reflection as "an intimate date with yourself."

These moments offer opportunities to make peace with the past: to assess where we are, how we got there, and cleanse our psyche of frustrations or unwarranted judgments we may be making about ourselves. They are also occasions to focus on our future. They give us the chance to connect with a vision, set goals, create action plans, build confidence, and commit to taking action.

Personal planning drives continuous improvement in our performance. The key to it is the rhythm at which we take these timeouts so that we have high quality self-reflections, uncovering helpful insights about our lives. Occasionally, we find ourselves in the perfect state of mind for such introspection, outside of our planned reflection time. These moments are opportunities to be seized, as they can yield some of the most profound insights.

If we prefer a more structured approach, we can engage in these planning sessions at various frequencies—whether daily, weekly, monthly, quarterly, yearly, or any combination. Each one helps us reground and reposition ourselves in distinct ways. A daily time-out may simply involve a quick review of that day's to-do list and making a plan for the next day. A weekly reflection could be more elaborate, while a yearly one would focus on a longer time horizon and broader perspective. Each of us will determine the approach that works best for us.

In the next section, I share my planning practices to serve as thought starters for shaping an individualized approach. Before that, I will highlight four principles which I believe help in creating plans which truly drive personal performance.

The first concerns being selective in goal-setting. We have many roles in life, which can lead to more ideas for goal-setting than we can realistically focus on. Added to this are self-focused goals such as those for our well-being, career, finances, skills, or relationships. When combined with role-specific goals, the list can quickly become overwhelming. Maintaining discipline in prioritization is crucial for reaping the benefits of personal planning.

Second, the time horizon for our goals is also important. Disparate short-term goals will keep us busy, tire us out and, over time, degrade our performance. When we set goals with a long-term perspective and recognize the progress we make toward them, we will feel more productive, less tired, and our accomplishments will carry more significance. Clearly, short-term goals will always be a part of our plans. The key is to remain mindful that they aren't the only goals to pursue and that, to the extent possible, they contribute to accomplishing our long-term aspirations.

Third, contrary to the conventional wisdom that goals must be objectively measurable, we can benefit from being more flexible in personal planning. Some goals for our growth may not lend themselves to objective measurement. It is still better to set such goals, even if we gauge them subjectively.

For instance, a goal to eradicate a mental habit of assuming pessimistic scenarios can be hard to measure objectively. Yet, by tuning in to our emotions, taking notes, and reviewing those notes from time to time, we can track our progress toward this goal. This raises our awareness of the habit and, eventually, can help us get rid of this knee-jerk pessimism.

Finally, our human ecosystem can play an important role. Sometimes, self-reflection alone isn't enough to reground and reposition ourselves in a way which recharges us. We might need the wisdom and support of others to come to terms with the past, build belief in our ability to make a difference, set the right expectations of ourselves, or develop the right action plans. Reaching out to those we trust is a great way to enrich our planning.

FINDING YOUR RHYTHM

The origins of my ideas on personal planning go back to the early years in my career where the companies I worked for required annual performance reviews. These reviews typically began with a self-assessment—comparing your performance to a plan which you had previously submitted. Initially, preparing yearly performance plans wasn't an exciting part of my job; I only did so because it was required. It seemed to me that was also the case for most people completing or reviewing them.

Later on, I decided to trust the idea that planning could improve my performance and began preparing my plans more thoughtfully. At first, that deeper thinking was difficult. The plans I produced didn't seem to have a significant impact on my performance, although I did notice some improvements. As I kept up the habit, I began to see more meaningful effects. Eventually, I became so convinced of its benefits that I extended this planning process to other areas of my life. Let's walk through how I now do it.

I find a week to be a great unit of time for useful reflections on my performance. When I take a weekly timeout, I start by questioning myself on what I call, "the three *P*'s":

- Have I made the progress I intended to make?
- Have I remained positive?
- Have I worked efficiently; in other words, was I productive?

I grade myself on each *P* every week to jog my memory. Some weeks, that grading may only take a few seconds, but in others I may need to think more deeply; especially when I award myself a lower grade than I like or when I think my performance exceeded my expectations.

During one of my weekly reflections, frustrated by constantly missing progress goals I had set for *Soulgery,* I paused to consider why this might be happening. As I was tracking my time—the topic of the next chapter—I was able to find a useful answer. Analyzing the numbers, I made an interesting discovery: whenever I spent around 20 hours on *Soulgery,* I made far more progress.

In another weekly timeout, I realized that even when I did put in the 20 hours, I still had weeks where I was missing my progress goals. I then decided to focus on the way I was writing as a possible source of the problem. That led to another interesting discovery. I realized that I had a tendency to jump too quickly to writing instead of taking the right amount of time to think through the context of the content, to be crystal clear about the main idea and the best flow to convey it. Once I started off by doing that, I became more fluid.

In weeks when my emotions run high, I take time to reflect more on the second *P*—my positivity. This helps me become more balanced when I feel I have become unduly pessimistic. The Hindu sage Ramana Maharishi is often quoted as saying: "Thoughts come and go. Feelings come and go. Find out what it is that remains." I try to take that advice further and decide what I *want* to remain in my world of thoughts and emotions; to recognize and channel my emotions to more useful ends, to connect, build on, or discard the thoughts which keep dancing in my mind. (See chapter 14 for more detailed discussions on managing emotions.)

I can't claim that I am always successful in doing this, but the exercise helps me recognize any destructive thoughts or emotions I may be harboring. This awareness acts like a shield to protect me from getting into a worse mood the following week. It also feels like I have cleansed and organized my thoughts, at least partially.

Whenever I feel like I've had an unproductive day, I briefly pause at the end of it to reflect on the reasons why—whether it's a lack of discipline, low energy, or distractions. I then take quick actions to address whatever has caused it. Most importantly, I strengthen my resolve to make the next day more productive. I revisit this third *P*—my productivity—during the next weekly reflection.

I then shift my focus to the future and produce a weekly plan which guides me during the week and serves as the basis for that week's evaluation. These weekly plans are connected to a yearly plan which I produce through a similar process: first evaluating my annual performance, and then setting goals and creating action plans for the following year. The yearly plans, in turn, are guided by my long-term vision, which I revisit each year.

Once or twice a year, I step back and look at my performance over longer periods of time. On one of those occasions, I noticed how, generally, I am at my best in the first quarter of the year, that I somehow drop off a little in the second quarter, try to recover in the third, and really struggle in the fourth—mostly because I don't have the same energy level as I usually have in the first quarter.

This pattern has been happening for some years, but I wasn't doing anything about it, other than attributing it to factors beyond my control like seasonal changes or distractions during the summer. Seeing this pattern in the numbers moved me to action. I started thinking about how I could sustain peak performance throughout the year. This actually made it into my list of goals for the following year.

Through pacing myself, becoming smarter about how I worked, exercising, being thoughtful about my diet, and managing my frustrations better, I was able to impact my performance positively for the other quarters.

In setting goals, I often go against my own advice. Recently, I set a total of 22 goals for just one year. Halfway through that year, I realized that 3 of them were goals I should have never set. It was also clear that I would definitely miss 6 because I hadn't even begun to work on them. As for the remaining 13, I achieved some and made good progress on the others.

Sometimes, I use goal-setting as a way to build resilience. All of us experience what I call "fall times." Those are the periods when we feel our state of being is not as we would wish. We are weighed down by negativity, our minds become cluttered, or we don't seem to care about anything.

Goal setting helps me recover from those periods. When I declare a fall time to myself, I prioritize two goals. First, to get back to a better state of mind sooner than I had in previous fall times, and second, to get through this fall time with minimal damage. Often, just being aware that I am in a fall time helps get me back up before too long. Sometimes, I may have to take a rest, pace myself for a while, go back to regular physical activity, talk to friends and family, or set aside more time for reflection.

The fall times I experienced during the earlier periods in my career could last weeks or even months. Later on, as I started setting goals, I was able to get back up more quickly. As my full-time executive career drew to a close, I was setting goals to recover by the next day. I even experimented with the idea of recovering from a bad meeting before the next one started.

Over the years, I have become convinced that planning is a key intervention to improve my performance. I follow routines but I also remain flexible so that I can leverage opportunities for quality self-reflection.

Finding our rhythm for personal planning is like learning to ride a bike. You get on it, start pedaling, and keep it up until maintaining balance becomes second nature. We start this by making two decisions. The first is to choose the life roles we include in the scope of our planning. The second is to determine the frequency of our timeouts. Keeping a critical eye on what works and what doesn't, and continually evolving our approach will help us settle into a rhythm, setting in motion one of the key drivers for performing with excellence. In the next chapter we will talk about another: managing our time.

12

MANAGING TIME

Time is a storm in which we are all lost.

—William Carlos Williams, *The Descent, The Desert Music and Other Poems,* 1954

The average life expectancy for us humans is less than eight decades. The first one passes with limited consciousness and decision-making. The last one depends on our well-being. So, all in all, what we have, on average, is 6–7 decades. What we call life, is that time.

In pursuit of performance excellence, time is a key resource to manage. It is a finite, non-renewable, and scarce resource. Once used up, we can't make or buy more of it. Its availability is uncertain; at any point in time, we don't know how much of it we have left. If anything in life deserves to be well managed, it has to be time.

Managing any resource effectively requires knowing how much of it has been used and for what purpose. Yet, as precious a resource as time is, the idea of tracking it isn't so appealing. Even when we constantly face competing priorities and lack sufficient time for important activities, tracking time rarely comes to mind as a way to the solution. I discovered its value through an idea that I came across during a developmental program.

This program was held in an operating unit of a company where we had a chance to engage with people from all departments, at all levels of the hierarchy. What was immediately evident in the culture of this company was that they were truly market driven. Leaders in market-facing functions were expected to spend at least 80 percent of their time in the marketplace, including the CEO.

At the end of the program, the CEO's final words to us were: if you take nothing else home, at least remember the 80 percent rule. I took this advice to heart, but didn't think I could spend 80 percent of my time in the marketplace. I thought I could reach 60 percent and committed to doing that. I tracked my time to honor that commitment.

This practice quickly revealed its value. As I began to spend that proportion of time in the marketplace, I started recognizing many benefits. I was building great connections with our teams and customers, seeing reality as it was, rather than only through reports. Additionally, I had the chance to perpetuate the cultural traits I valued to a greater audience than before.

The insight of consistently spending a majority of time in the marketplace proved to be effective. Tracking my time allowed me to act on it with objectivity and discipline, amplifying the value of this insight. It also pushed me to be more innovative and efficient in the way I worked. As it reinforced my sense of purpose and heightened my intensity, I started to notice significant improvements in my performance.

I kept up the habit for as long as I was in that role, but I didn't track my time in my subsequent executive roles. I felt the diligence I developed in planning my work was good enough to ensure I was spending my time in the right way. Looking back, I now feel a bit circumspect about that decision, especially after having experienced the benefits of doing it in my post-executive life. I shared some examples of those in the previous chapter.

Tracking time is like opening a window on a cool morning: you might not think it is needed at first, but once fresh air flows in, it brings a sense of renewal and clarity. Similarly, when considering how to pursue our aspirations, we often don't reflect deeply enough on how much time our tasks require and how they fit into the rest of our lives. By tracking time, we gain a clear and objective perspective on what we can reasonably take on, enabling us to move forward with purpose and discipline.

As a side note, tracking time isn't a cumbersome exercise at all. If you already schedule your time on an electronic calendar, you can find an application which calculates the hours you spent based on that calendar. It takes me five minutes—or less—each week to track and report the time I have spent.

Knowing where our time goes is one part of managing this precious resource. How well we use it is the other. Using time well means being efficient and effective with it: spending it on the "right" objectives and performing tasks in the shortest possible time. In everyday language, it is about doing more with the time we have. That "more" can be the quantity of what we achieve, or its significance.

Businesses are always challenged to do more with what they have, or even less. They try to rise to that challenge by eliminating waste, changing the way they work, and doubling down on what really matters. By anchoring their decisions on a long-term direction, they find ways of doing more with less, ultimately becoming stronger in the process.

At a fundamental level, we can approach managing our time in a similar way. We, too, can eliminate waste, change the way we operate, and double down on what really matters. If we make our decisions with a long-term perspective, we will also do more with less and grow in the process.

We will cover two of these ideas in this chapter. First, we will explore the concept of eliminating waste through simplifying. Next, we will present a perspective on evaluating the way we operate in our various roles to enhance our efficiency and effectiveness. As for doubling down on what really matters, one part of this is the discipline of prioritization which we covered in the previous chapter. The other part is to maximize the value of our time by amplifying our intentionality. That is discussed in the next chapter.

SIMPLIFYING

Throughout my executive life, I sought to simplify the concept of leadership, which was not only my responsibility, but also a fascination. I believed that simplifying it would help me stay more focused and perform more effectively.

Leadership has been the subject of countless writings, and nearly all perspectives hold relevance in some context. This makes the task of simplification difficult. In one of my first attempts, I distilled the essence of leadership into seven tough questions:

1. Do I believe?
2. Do I care?
3. Am I realistic?
4. Do I make tough decisions?
5. Do I have inner strength?
6. Am I approachable?
7. Do I develop myself?

The first two questions address foundational qualities of leadership: belief and care—for the business, the strategy, the team, and myself. The third question concerns setting realistic expectations, and making sound judgments about people, strategies, and relationships. The fourth question—making tough decisions—is perhaps the most consequential. When faced with high stakes, am I capable of remaining grounded, taking decisive action, and doing the right thing, even when it is inconvenient? The last three questions focus on personal traits that I believe distinguish a leader.

I left out a number of leadership qualities in the interest of simplicity. For example, the word *integrity* is not on this list—not because it is unimportant, but because it is indirectly covered by the other questions, such as making tough decisions or being approachable. Similarly, the questions don't explicitly address leadership accountabilities like creating a vision, fostering an empowering culture, or being a role model. I felt that focusing on the seven questions would naturally lead me to reflect on these. For instance, caring for the business will naturally lead to envisioning a better future for it; or, in order to believe in the strategy, it first has to be created.

By comparing these seven questions to other leadership frameworks, one might identify features that I didn't consider. That may well be the case, but for me, the key point was that this exercise in simplification sharpened my focus and allowed me to direct my time and energy more purposefully.

In a conversation I had with a friend, I mentioned this idea of seven questions as a way of thinking about leadership. Before I could ask the first question, he said that more than three concepts at a time was too much for him to take on board. I didn't think he was saying that because he lacked the capacity to understand more than three concepts at a time. I interpreted it as a subtle call for further simplification.

I took that challenge to heart and sought to deliver on it in *Soulgery* by describing a growth model that introduces no more than three concepts at a time, or less. While there were some exceptions—like the Four Acts of Growth—embracing this challenge helped me navigate the complexity of various topics. It also forced me to focus my time on the ideas that mattered the most. By simplifying, I could avoid unnecessary distractions, and ultimately created a model I felt confident in.

Simplification is relevant for anything we do—the way we think, act, solve problems, and communicate. It is a refined skill that helps us eliminate clutter and capture the essence of matters. Leonardo da Vinci refers to simplicity as "the ultimate sophistication."

Anyone can develop this skill by practicing it—whether in solving a problem, understanding a complex situation, or communicating a difficult concept. This practice is about taking time to challenge ourselves with questions such as:

- Have I understood why it matters?
- What part of it is unnecessary or unimportant?
- Can I think about it differently?
- Can I say it clearly, briefly, and understandably?

As we practice this mental habit, simplifying becomes intrinsic to how we operate, helping us become more efficient and effective with our time.

In his 1657 work "Lettres Provinciales," ("The Provincial Letters") French philosopher and mathematician Blaise Pascal wrote: "I have made this letter longer than usual, because I lack the time to make it short." It does take time to simplify, but it's an investment with rich returns—both in the form of better use of our time and gaining greater wisdom.

EVOLVING HOW WE OPERATE

Each of us has a way of operating in our different roles, whether we have chosen it consciously or not. By periodically reviewing this, just as businesses do, we can improve our efficiency and effectiveness.

The most basic element of how we function is the way we organize ourselves. Are we able to find what we need when we need it? In an increasingly digital world, where the volume and speed of information can overwhelm us, this has become even more important.

In one of my yearly reflections, I came up with an idea of organizing all documents, emails, and notes around my life taxonomy—a hierarchical structure that includes everything I do in life. As I used it, I saw improvements in my productivity. When I shared this idea with a colleague, he responded by saying that a less sophisticated approach works for him. He simply uses the search function in his different apps to find what he needs. While this made me question whether my idea was actually complicating my life, I decided to stick with it.

Clearly, what works for one may not work for another. Yet, all of us can benefit from occasionally reviewing the way we are organized. The improvements we make as a result can free up time for more appealing pursuits.

The processes we follow also define the way we operate. Whatever we produce—whether it's a report, a speech, or a decision—comes out of a process. While a particular process might have become second nature, it quietly underpins our actions, influencing the outcomes. By becoming more conscious of our processes and keeping a critical eye on them, we can enhance our performance.

During one of my weekly reflections, I decided to focus on the process I used to prepare for important meetings. While I typically allocate ample time for these, I identified some areas for improvement and developed a 3-step process that has proven highly effective. The process is straightforward.

The first step is to focus on the big picture, which includes the goals, the agenda, the stakeholder landscape, and a high-level review of the topics involved. The second step is to review these topics in detail. Finally, the third step is to write a summary of takeaways before the meeting. This new process enhances my preparation by sharpening my focus on the bigger picture both at the beginning and the end. I find that when I follow this process, I consistently perform my role to my satisfaction.

We can also benefit from reviewing how we approach seemingly minor tasks that still consume our time. For example, going through one's inbox isn't a terribly important activity, but in my case, when my inbox is crowded, it weighs me down in a strange way. I feel that I am being left behind or losing control, creating a haze in my mind which I am sure hinders my performance.

Clearly, a quick solution would be to get rid of this thought pattern, but I just couldn't do that. My desire for clarity and control has always been too strong. That eventually led me to devise a process that would provide both.

Every day, I go through my inbox, taking one of four actions with each message: respond to those which are urgent or quick to deal with; file away those which can wait a week in a folder labeled "current," which I clean up at the end of a week; and file away those which don't need a response, but which I wish to keep. I delete any message which doesn't fall into any of those categories. That filing is, of course, in line with my life taxonomy.

At the height of activity during my executive life, this process allowed me to have no more than 10 messages in my inbox at day's end. That helped me to be as responsive as I wanted, while remaining informed. The more important benefit was the sense of comfort and control over my work which allowed me to better focus on what is truly important.

Reviewing the way we operate with a process lens will improve both our efficiency and effectiveness. With rapid advances in AI, we have greater opportunities to radically transform our processes. We will be better served by integrating those developments into our lives sooner rather than later.

Finally, a third dimension which defines the way we operate is the balance we strike between planning and spontaneity.

We previously discussed planning in terms of the legacies we wish to create, and then as a way to continually improve our performance. The concepts we discussed in those chapters apply equally to any work we do. Yet, how far we take this idea is for each one of us to determine. If our plans don't help us perform our work any better, maybe we should cut down on them? On the other hand, if we frequently find ourselves running out of time, being caught off guard, or having coordination issues, better planning will undoubtedly help.

Plans and processes generally make us more productive, but they can also limit us if they cause us to lose our spontaneity. Like performing artists, our best performances are often spontaneous ones.

A quote attributed to Oscar Wilde suggests: "Spontaneity is a meticulously prepared art." This reminds us that true spontaneity doesn't necessarily emerge from chaos but from a solid foundation of preparation. Personal planning, evaluating our processes, and organizing ourselves are essential to building that foundation. When the energy of an interaction flows in an unexpected direction, confidently stepping away from our plans and processes allows us to embrace spontaneity and discover its beauty.

Each cornerstone of the way we work—whether it's how we organize, the processes we follow, or the balance we strike between planning and spontaneity—helps us enhance our productivity. When paired with a commitment to continuously improve our ability to simplify, they empower us to fully harness this most precious resource: time.

The Puzzle

In this chapter and the previous one, we explored two interlocking pieces of the performance excellence puzzle: personal planning and time management. Personal planning guides how we allocate time, while time management provides the discipline to follow that plan, helping us become more efficient and effective.

Another crucial benefit of diligent time management is gaining a realistic perspective on our limits. Just as insufficient funds can ground a business plan in reality, understanding our time constraints forces us to recognize what we can reasonably take on, helping us strike the right balance between ambition and realism.

Together, personal planning and time management lay the groundwork for us to perform with excellence. Yet, excellence comes to life at the moment of truth—in the performance itself. In the next chapter, we explore how we can prepare for that moment.

13

PERFORMING FOR IMPACT

Victorious warriors win first and then go to war, while defeated warriors go to war first and then seek to win.

—Sun Tzu, *The Art of War*

Achieving performance excellence mirrors Sun Tzu's insight: with careful preparation, we can secure success long before the performance itself. Let's delve into what this preparation entails and how it sets the foundation for victory.

Most of our preparation for a performance focuses on mastering the subject matter—a vital foundation. Yet true excellence in performance depends just as much on the state of our psyche at the moment we perform. Preparing for this mental state is at least as important as mastering the subject matter. While performing artists may have coaches to help them prepare psychologically, we—the performing artists of life—have to do that ourselves.

One of the cornerstones of psychological readiness is the strength of our intentionality. A quote that is often attributed to George Leonard, a notable proponent of the human potential movement suggests: "Ultimately, human intentionality is the most powerful force on this planet." Intentions act as energy; once felt by our audience—whether a group or an individual—they position us for a high-impact performance. Cultivating this energy within ourselves is an essential part of preparing for our important performances.

The vitality of this energy comes from what genuinely drives us in a performance. External motivators such as career advancement, financial rewards, or reputation can inspire effort, but they often fall short in bringing out our best. Our greatest performances unfold when we are driven by intrinsic motivators: a deep care for what we do, a sense of purpose, the passion to leave a legacy, or a commitment to our own high standards. Each performance offers an opportunity to activate, rekindle, or deepen these motivators. By reflecting deliberately on them during preparation, we cultivate the kind of intentionality that fuels excellence.

We can amplify our intentionality with a vision of success, particularly when that vision centers on the impact we aim to make on our audience. This drives excellence in two ways. First, the vision itself activates us with a sense of purpose and direction. Second, the process of envisioning our impact compels us to understand our audience more deeply, enabling us to engage with them meaningfully during the performance.

Another cornerstone of psychological readiness is our overall inner strength. Over the years, I have often witnessed brutal exploitation of inner weaknesses—whether during a business presentation, a negotiation, or even a simple conversation. A lack of confidence, overconfidence, presence of worry, or fear leaves a "smell of blood in the water" which others are quick to detect and exploit.

Additionally, external distractions can strike at the moment of truth—unnerving comments, unpleasant surprises, or a thick air of negativity—all threatening to throw us off-balance just as we are about to perform. Our best defense for fending off these distractions is to remain inwardly strong and grounded in our vision.

The challenge, however, is that the constant demands of daily life—stress, fatigue and emotional setbacks—erode our inner strength without us even realizing it. We can counter this by dedicating part of our preparation time to fostering a winner's mindset—focused, resolute, and confident—and committing to maintain that stance when it matters most. These lay the second cornerstone for psychological readiness.

Finally, the third cornerstone is our ability to appeal to both the minds and hearts of our audiences. While subject matter expertise helps us connect with their minds, what elevates communication to a higher level of impact is connecting with their hearts. To quote Rumi: "If words come from the heart, they will go to the heart. If they come from the tongue, they will not pass beyond the ears."

Among the many skills and techniques for impactful communication, I believe the ability to speak from the heart is paramount. This comes naturally when we feel a deep connection to the subject matter. We can also cultivate this connection through intentional reflection, uncovering what deeply resonates within us. Focusing on our intentionality—as discussed earlier in this chapter—also strengthens this bond, making our communication more authentic and powerful. Taking the time for this kind of introspection allows us to deliver a message that moves beyond logic and speaks directly to emotions. When our love, passion, and belief resonate with our audience, our impact becomes penetrating and energizing.

Building psychological readiness for performance excellence is as crucial as mastering the subject matter itself, if not more so. Allowing sufficient time for this preparation and using that time well is how, in the words of Sun Tzu, we can be the warriors who win before going to war.

HARVESTING LEARNINGS

Our performances are rich with lessons. Each one tells a story, with a setting, a history, characters, a plot, an ending, and consequences. Insights can emerge at any point. By reflecting on why and how events unfolded, we gain new wisdom, learn about others, and ourselves. While preparing our psyche is critical for more important performances, lessons can be drawn from any performance, even those we deem unimportant. One such experience for me was when I had to coordinate the resolution of an administrative issue.

I do not particularly enjoy dealing with administrative matters. So, when this issue first came up, my initial reaction was to rush through it. I quickly wrote an email explaining the situation, proposing a solution, and asking for feedback. One of the responses I got really irritated me. I found subtle notes of criticisms expressed in a lecturing style. I was already frustrated that I had to deal with this issue. The email added annoyance to that frustration. That got me to a point of wanting to kill off the issue with another quick email, which I tried to do.

A few days later, I looked at both of the emails I had written and realized I had missed some important facts about the situation. After further back and forth, I ended up accepting the view proposed in that annoying email, which didn't feel very good. Acting before fully understanding came at a price.

While this coordination exercise wasn't a significant performance for me, I felt irritated by the whole situation and took some time to reflect on the experience. I wanted to be clear with myself on why I became so annoyed and performed poorly. On reflection, I concluded that it really had to do with how I handled criticism. I recognized that I handle constructive criticism well, but not necessarily other kinds. The annoyance I felt in that email I received activated my sense of self. In a split second, it was asking me to do something to protect it. I responded to that request with those two emails, both of which had a combative tone.

Once I realized that this was another case of an impulse to serve my sense of self, the anger I had felt dissipated. In fact, it turned into a key learning: when we believe others' actions aren't well intended, it becomes much harder to recognize how we are driven to preserve our sense of self. In such moments, our minds tend to fixate on what others are doing to us. If we can get over this tendency and remain sharply focused on our own mistakes—even when others' intentions aren't pure—we will have achieved an important milestone in managing our sense of self.

The discipline to prepare for our performances and a commitment to learn from them are critical to delivering excellence. Naturally, some performances carry greater importance and therefore merit more thoughtful and thorough preparation. It is up to each of us to determine the level of preparation needed for a given performance. Similar to our discussions on personal planning, this is also a matter of finding our individual rhythm that leads to excellence in the moment of truth.

We will now move into the final piece of the performance excellence puzzle: our overall well-being.

14

INVESTING IN CORE

Flowers need water to blossom; so do you.

—Anonymous

During one of our extended family gatherings, filled with joy and steeped in the scent of delicious Turkish food, I found myself drawn into a conversation about a doctor who practiced alternative medicine. The stories I was hearing were bordering on the miraculous. As I listened to these extraordinary tales, I was captivated by this doctor's unconventional interventions. More than mere curiosity, a keen interest in the natural and holistic remedies he offered began to take root in me.

My intrigue prompted me to pay a visit just to learn about his practice, even though I didn't have any health complaints at the time. In his office, filled with numerous artifacts that radiated a mystical aura, he started the first session by "listening" to my pulse with his fingers. After 15 minutes or so, he began to review my vital signs with me, which he gauged solely by feeling my pulse. To my surprise, his readings were pretty accurate.

He then asked me what had happened to my left knee. I initially couldn't recall anything about it. A few weeks later, however, with my awareness sparked by that question, I began to notice that when I stayed on my feet for too long, I would feel a slight ache on the back of my left knee. I then remembered that I had injured my left toe some years before, and that ache in my left knee was probably a chain reaction in my body, compensating for that initial injury.

This is a typical case of the *creeping normality effect.*[1] We can get used to small and gradual changes in our body and accept what we have as normal, until those changes turn into problems. In this case, I was fortunate to become aware of it before it turned into a more serious problem.

He went on to give me his diagnosis of what was wrong with me. Nothing he said indicated an immediate threat to my health. His advice sounded like optional measures to improve my overall functioning. For example, he mentioned some issues with my gut, which he said was the cause of my suboptimal sleep quality and occasional fluctuations in my blood pressure. As I listened, I remembered that I had once fainted and woke up vomiting while on a flight because of my blood pressure tanking. Without that reminder, that unpleasant memory would have easily remained forgotten—another case of creeping normality.

At the end of the check-up, he recommended a 30-day regimen, which involved acupuncture, massage, a variety of other treatments, and a nutritional program. I wanted to do this to see what would happen, but the time required made me pause. I figured, with the horrendous traffic in Istanbul, each visit would take at least three hours. I thought I should do this at a more convenient time. It was easy to justify postponing it, as I didn't have any immediate health concerns and had a heavy schedule including lots of travel. Yet, it was hard to tell when there would ever be a convenient time.

As the doctor sensed I was thinking this way, he immediately intervened. He said that as my system was under strain, time wouldn't heal it, that it would only get worse. So, the earlier I fixed it, the better. His intervention worked. I decided to go ahead with the 30-day program.

---

[1] A term used by American scientist Jared Diamond in his 2005 book *Collapse: How Societies Choose to Fail or Succeed.*

Two weeks into the treatment, I already started feeling the benefits. My sleep quality improved, my energy increased, and even my mental agility got better, making me more effective at work. By the time I had finished the treatment, I felt as if I was at a completely different level of well-being. Having seen these benefits, I decided to continue visiting him on a weekly basis, just to get a reset or a tune-up after a busy workweek.

Over our 20+ year relationship, we became close friends, and I completed many long regimens like the first one. During that time, I witnessed many times what one could call a miracle, including some I have personally benefited from. His passing away left a void in my life. Not only had I lost a friend, but also a practitioner in whose hands I entrusted my well-being. I am not sure if I will ever replace the combination of him and what he called Tibetan medicine.

As I understand it, the philosophy of Tibetan medicine is to activate the body to heal itself rather than attack a problem directly. It involves a holistic understanding, identifying how different points in the body relate to different organs, and how energy flows through the meridians to keep us vibrant. That approach, combined with his unique gift for recognizing issues—well before modern medicine could—offered me the perfect opportunity to proactively manage my well-being.

Although it's unlikely that I will ever be able to fill the void created by the passing away of my doctor friend, I believe the three lessons I learned in those 20+ years will positively impact my health in the years to come.

First, I realized that even though I am not a medical expert, I can take a more active leadership role in managing my well-being. This is akin to how a CEO leads a company. You don't have to be an expert in every function to lead a business. Just as a CEO relies on a strong team, managing our well-being also requires the right support network.

I have learned that being open to diverse perspectives and approaches, especially alternative medicine, can make a significant difference in building this team. Alternative medicine often draws skepticism, but my experience has shown me that just because something hasn't been scientifically tested doesn't mean it can't be effective. In other words, absence of evidence is not evidence of absence. Many medical approaches, practiced for centuries, may lack a scientific evidential basis yet still offer valuable insights into our bodies and methods for preventive care. They can complement the essential role of modern medicine in managing our well-being.

Fitness instructors, nutritional counselors, or life coaches form key members of this support network, each bringing expertise to specific areas of well-being. Managing this diverse team requires an integrative approach, where the ability to listen to our bodies plays a central role. Much like a CEO synthesizes input from various team members before making a final decision, managing our health involves blending expert advice with informed judgment to determine what works best for us.

Second, this experience proved to me that believing we don't have time for nurturing our well-being is merely an illusion. My initial reaction—that I had to wait for a better time to start the 30-day regimen—offers proof of this. Once I made the decision to commit, I found ways to make time. If my travel schedule didn't allow for 30 straight days, it was fine to do 14 consecutive days to start, then 2–3 days per week to finish it. I carved out the three hours I needed each day by cutting back on long dinners and going to bed earlier.

The third lesson I took from this is that the key to maintaining our overall vibrancy is to adopt a holistic *and* preventive approach. By striving to understand our bodies as a whole and implementing timely preventive care, we can address many health issues before they become significant problems. Given our mysteries and complexities, developing a holistic view of our bodies and learning to act in a timely fashion will always be a challenge. However, despite the unknowns, fundamentals such as exercise, sleep, nutrition, managing stress, and practicing moderation can significantly contribute to well-being.

A holistic approach to well-being goes beyond the physical. Our overall vibrancy also depends on managing our thoughts and emotions, as well as connecting with our spirituality. In the next two sections, we will explore these two topics in more depth.

MANAGING OUR EMOTIONS

Emotions are like energy. We can't eliminate them, nor do they disappear when we suppress or ignore them. As to what we can do with them, this passage from Rumi, titled "The Guest House," as translated by Coleman Barks, offers guidance:

> This being human is a guest house.
> Every morning is a new arrival.
> A joy, a depression, a meanness, some momentary awareness comes as an unexpected visitor.
> Welcome and entertain them all.
> Treat each guest honorably.
> The dark thought, the shame, the malice, meet them at the door laughing, and invite them in.
> Be grateful for whoever comes, because each has been sent as a guide from beyond.

This beautiful metaphor of the guest house reminds us that emotions are not to be resisted but welcomed with curiosity and grace. By treating them as guides, we can first reflect on the purpose they serve and then channel them toward that purpose, transforming them into fuel for meaningful action. After all, doesn't each emotion have a purpose to fulfill?

Anger can be useful because it gives us power. When we are angry, we feel more confident and capable. If that power is directed to the right end, it can create positive change. The key, though, is to get rid of it once it has served its purpose—just like the calm that follows the storm. Expressed that way and directed toward the right thing, anger becomes useful.

The emotion of worry probably exists to prompt us to take necessary precautions for our safety. We can channel its energy into considering what we might have overlooked, addressing the source of our concern. Worrying beyond that serves no purpose.

An interesting emotion is irritation. A quote which is commonly attributed to Carl Jung suggests: "Everything that irritates you about others leads to an understanding of the self." If we can direct the energy of irritation inward, questioning ourselves, maybe we will discover some of our own dark spots. Years ago, I remember being constantly irritated by the behavior of a certain individual. That was until I finally recognized that the reason for my irritation was a feeling of jealousy. It wasn't easy for me to confront this, but once I had done so, the jealousy and the irritation ebbed away.

When we try to work with an emotion in this way, we rewire ourselves. Next time the same stimulus arrives, we won't have the same emotional reaction.

It may not be easy to channel our emotions toward a useful purpose in real time. Sometimes, the best we can do is to park it so that it doesn't get in our way as much. That emotion will show up again in some other context and that's a good thing. It gives us the opportunity to keep working on making it useful. As we keep training our muscles for channeling our emotions toward their intended purpose, over time, we will be able to adjust more quickly and, perhaps, even in real time.

Emotions seem to be less easy to control than our thoughts, yet they exert more control over us. Actively managing them in this way will give us a better command over our psyche. We will also be able to experience emotions without being fully captivated by them and learn to leverage their power.

CONNECTING WITH OUR SPIRITUALITY

In my 20+ years' experience with my doctor friend, I sensed that elements of spirituality were at play. The way he conducted himself during the treatments made me think that spirituality is not only a phenomenon beyond this world; it reveals itself in our daily lives as well. This led me to wonder if I could have similar spiritual experiences outside of his clinic.

I began paying closer attention to moments when I felt inspired, in a state of flow, or experienced a mystical connection. I reckoned that if I could understand how I reached these states, I might be able to connect with my spirituality more often. I vividly recall one of my walks along the Bosphorus in İstanbul priming me for such a discovery.

These walks were highly productive. I always carried a smartphone to capture important ideas that came to mind. On one of my walks, I decided that I should not interrupt my flow by taking notes. My ambitious self, however, couldn't tolerate the possibility that good ideas might come up and be forgotten. In the end, my flow-seeking self and my ambitious self agreed to meet each other halfway: I would take a mental note of good ideas. So, off I went.

As I walked, I took mental notes on three ideas which I considered important. Unfortunately, proving my ambitious self correct, by the time I returned home, I could remember only two of them. I kept pushing myself to remember that third point, but to no avail. I decided to get on with the day. I took a shower and then moved on to my morning prayer. For me prayers are meditative exercises where I try to cleanse my mind. In this case, that included the frustration of having forgotten the third idea. Magically, as I finished my prayer the third point gently floated into my mind from somewhere beyond.

That seemingly insignificant experience raised a question: was this the work of my spiritual dimension or something else? I can't say whether it was or wasn't. Yet, the experience had all the characteristics of a spiritual experience. I felt as if I was connected to something greater. It happened because I entered a state of calm. When the third idea showed up, without thinking about it, I sent a heartfelt gratitude to wherever that help had come from.

Experiences like feeling inspired, being in a state of flow, or serendipity, are a part of life. We can call that our spiritual dimension, our mysterious part, or something else. Whatever we call it, we can experience this dimension more frequently by trying to notice it and by responding to it with gratitude. That can be a way of inviting our spiritual dimension into our everyday lives. As we do so, it gradually becomes a natural part of our consciousness. We may then begin trusting it and tap into more of its capacity to inspire us, spark our imagination, and make us more intuitive.

IN PURSUIT OF A UTOPIA

We are like fertile gardens. On the one hand, we can beautifully flourish when we tend to ourselves with care, wisdom, and discipline. On the other, just as weeds and pests can silently overtake a garden, that creeping normality effect can trap us into becoming lesser versions of ourselves.

Just as CEOs lead their companies with a vision, being the CEO of our well-being also calls for us to have a clear vision for it. That vision can have elements such as:

- Being physically strong, agile, and flexible,
- Being intellectually curious, sharply cognitive, and engaged,
- Experiencing all emotions fully without getting captivated by them, and,
- Feeling wholeness within ourselves and with our environment.

This utopian vision can serve as the lodestar for our well-being. By relentlessly pursuing it with the help of our support network, we can discover the richness in our physical, intellectual, emotional, and spiritual selves and shield ourselves from the creeping normality effect.

Inevitably, there will come a point in life where we feel the vibrancy of our 4-D selves beginning to fade. Why does that happen? Is it due to aging, disease, or simply because we lose what we don't use? The correct answer is probably: all of the above.

Immortality isn't on the horizon yet. While Western medicine has made progress in reversing aging, we still have ways to go. We may prolong the vibrancy of our 4-D selves by deliberately remaining active with all of our dimensions—physically, emotionally, intellectually, and spiritually—but given the current state of affairs, decline will ultimately happen to us all.

Improving our well-being is always possible, until we decide it isn't any longer. When we make that decision, it is the time to accept reality and adjust. Until then, let's strive to be the best CEO of our well-being we can be.

• ACT 4 •

HACK YOUR GROWTH

15

THE DEFENSE GAME

To win, you must be daring enough to take the offensive and bold enough to maintain it.

—Napoleon Bonaparte

Life is like a strategy game where we play both offense and defense. So far in this book, we have focused on our offense game. Whether it's searching for meaning, making an impact, or pursuing excellence, we have the freedom to actively shape our path forward. Yet, much of life operates beyond our control, testing us with all kinds of adversities we didn't deliberately choose—conflicts to resolve, setbacks to endure, or changes that demand adaptation.

These challenges spare no one, pushing us out of our comfort zones, threatening our health, careers, finances, families, relationships, and inner peace. Some of them feel existential, while others strike when we already feel overwhelmed and tired. At times, we are faced with multiple daunting problems, all hitting us at once.

This is the defensive part of the game where we respond to what life does to us—a game of resilience, patience, and wisdom. It involves holding our ground, conserving energy, and preserving what's valuable. However, it is more than a passive game.

We have many options in dealing with challenges—ranging from quick fixes to lasting solutions. Our approach could be analytical, rational, emotional, or intuitive. We can choose to be forceful or subtle depending on the situation, learning through experience which levers to pull to improve our "success rate."

The key question, however, is this: can we emerge stronger from the adversities we face? This question is central to our defense game. Answering it affirmatively means we are building our capability and resilience for the challenges to come, preparing us to make a profound impact, even when life tests us with its greatest difficulties.

The next three chapters explore a growth-oriented approach to navigating adversity. We call this the 3R's method and discuss it in the following order:

1. Chapter 16: "Read it Right"—Reading our challenging situations thoroughly and constructively
2. Chapter 17: "Respond or React?"—Harnessing all resources available to us to overcome adversity
3. Chapter 18: "Reflect and Renew"—Renewing ourselves by "hacking" our default modes

The order of this discussion isn't intended to imply a strict sequence. On the contrary, this is a dynamic process where we constantly read an evolving situation and shape new responses. Along the way we discover fresh insights—into ourselves or the situations we face—allowing us to change course as necessary.

What makes the 3R's a growth-oriented approach are three underlying concepts: having a *smart bias for positivity,* being *prudently proactive,* and *sufficiently introspective.* These principles are the threads that weave through all discussions, empowering us to create new and inspiring realities out of the challenging situations we face and renewing ourselves in the process.

You might question whether such a growth-minded approach will be as effective in overcoming a particular challenge as one sharply focused on specific outcomes. The short answer is yes, provided we use the 3Rs pragmatically, deciding which parts are most relevant to a particular situation. Naturally, not all of the ideas presented will always be critical, but when used pragmatically and consistently, the 3R's have the potential to transform us through adversity.

In discussing human potential and growth, Abraham Maslow famously noted, "In any given moment, we have two options: to step forward into growth or to step back into safety." Our instinctive reaction to adversity might be to protect ourselves. Yet, a better approach is to treat our challenges like the seeds from which our better selves can emerge, growing naturally through the problems life throws our way.

16

READ IT RIGHT

You are confined only by the walls you build yourself.
—Andrew Murphy, Olympic athlete

Physics was my Achilles' heel at high school. The subject baffled me at every turn. Realizing I wouldn't have to face it in college was a source of relief. Little did I know, physics wasn't done with me yet. It would sneak back into my life in the most unexpected ways.

First, it came up in a dinner conversation at my maternal grandfather's home. While I lived and worked in İstanbul, Friday nights were always reserved for family dinners. A friend of mine who joined on one such occasion described the experience years later as one where you immediately felt warmth and love.

Often, there were deep discussions about life, which inevitably took us into the realms of religion and philosophy. It was on one such occasion that my grandfather talked about how the findings of quantum physics aligned with some of his religious beliefs. Unsurprisingly, my mental block about physics prevented me from understanding what he was saying. It did, though, pique my interest, but not so strongly that I would do anything about it.

Years later, I came across an article which talked about how a convergence was emerging in the view of reality presented by Sufism and quantum physics.

The article highlighted a number of parallels between them, some of which I couldn't fully understand, but two insights resonated deeply. One was the suggestion that the discovery of subatomic particles led to an understanding of the universe not as a collection of separate physical objects, but as a unified whole, containing a complex web of relations. The other was that this new view of reality can't be explained in ordinary language, as it lies beyond our sensory experiences. Both insights echoed the essence of Sufi thought as I had come to know it: the unity underlying apparent separation, and the truth that lies beyond words.

As my intrigue with quantum mechanics grew, I found myself drawing a parallel between its concept of *the observer effect* and the way we read the challenges we face. Simply put, the observer effect says that the act of observing or measuring a tiny particle, like an electron, can change its behavior. This principle can apply equally well to reading a situation.

At the core of our reading of any situation are the judgments we make. These can be about people's intentions, capabilities, how a situation unfolds, its potential outcomes, and what they mean to us. These judgments can actually alter the course of events. As a simple example, if we consider someone untrustworthy, and they sense that, they generally become more guarded in their engagement with us. They may even become suspicious or hostile. If, on the other hand, they receive more favorable vibes, in all likelihood they will respond with a more open and constructive attitude.

In dealing with adversity, we have the opportunity to make this observer effect work in our favor. That requires us to consider the effects of our judgments and opt for those which are more likely to help overcome our challenges. I call this *making judgments with a smart bias for positivity.*

BEING SMARTLY POSITIVE

A smart bias for positivity doesn't mean thinking of people or events as positive; nor is it about holding unrealistic expectations. It comes down to recognizing that both positives and negatives will always be there and keeping a sharp eye out for those positives—whether in ourselves, others, or in events. It is also about patiently and relentlessly digging them out and working with them in a constructive way.

Clearly, some of the judgments we make have to remain outside of the scope of such a bias. For example, it may be obvious from the onset that we are dealing with someone who shouldn't be trusted, no matter what. Yet, most of life is in the gray zone. We are often unable to make a definitive call, or we may not know the response we can elicit from others if we approach them positively. Opportunities lie in that gray zone. When we are there and make our judgments with a smart bias for positivity, we can make the observer effect work for us.

The smartness of this bias lies in knowing where and when positivity has no place. It also means being prepared for the consequences of the wrong judgments we might make. Finally, it involves remaining open to changing our views when new information emerges. Naturally, that smartness will evolve as we gain more experience. Along the way, others may misread us, or even take advantage of us.

Still, it is better to make our judgments with a smart bias for positivity, and learn from mistakes, rather than succumb to the abundance of negativity which surrounds the challenges we face. Allowing that negativity to dominate our psyche will certainly make the observer effect work against us and may even generate self-fulfilling prophecies.

Let's now talk about examples of how a smart bias for positivity can make the observer effect work in our favor. We will focus on three kinds of judgments we make that are often critical to reading a challenge: those we make on people's *intentions*, people's *capabilities*, and on the potential *outcomes*.

INTENTIONS—ABSENCE OF MALICE

I once had to deal with a set of existential issues involving a business in which the company I worked for held a minority stake. By the time I became involved with this company it had been performing badly for a long time. The shareholders had divergent views as to the best strategy to follow and the competence of management. As such, they could never agree on a road map to improve the performance of the business. The frustrations had built up over years, turning into deep mistrust amongst the shareholders.

Eventually, one of the shareholders decided to bring matters to a head and threatened legal action. In my first meeting with this shareholder, he conveyed in no uncertain terms that he was determined to stay on this path. That meant my company would be one of the defendants if the matter went to court.

In dealing with this challenge, one of the key decisions I had to take concerned the ultimate intent of this shareholder. Did he want to pacify the other shareholders and run the company himself, or was there still room in his mind for working together to improve the business? If I made the assumption that he would collaborate, could we really solve our problems?

Given everything that unfolded over the years, the prospect of working collaboratively wasn't immediately obvious. On our side of the conflict, the prevailing view was that working constructively with this shareholder would be very difficult, and interpreting his intentions positively seemed unwise.

Nonetheless, I didn't want to assume bad intent on his part before I had really experienced it. So I decided to give him the benefit of the doubt and tried to understand the situation from his perspective. After a few sessions, I came to understand why he had taken the actions he had. I also formed the view that, despite his legal threats, there was room in his mind for the idea of working together to improve the business. With this in mind, I chose to engage with him on that basis.

He responded positively, and we started working on a road map to resolve our issues. We eventually agreed on one which made improving the business the priority, leaving contentious issues between shareholders for a later date. The decisions we took helped improve the business and built trust. Over time, the performance of the business turned around, providing a strong platform to work on the other issues. Relationships among the different shareholders improved to a point where they no longer derailed performance.

People's intentions aren't necessarily fixed; they can be influenced by how we choose to engage with them. When the signs of danger are clear and abundant, assuming good intent can be counterintuitive. On the other hand, if we are too quick to assume bad intent, we risk not only missing opportunities to foster good intent but also risk inadvertently provoking the very negativity we fear. That certainly would have been the case in the example above.

It can also be the case with any other conflict or challenge we face—whether at work, at home, or in our communities. Going the extra mile, so as to be absolutely sure of bad intent, can sometimes be the catalyst for overcoming a challenge.

ABILITIES—MINDING THE GOOD

I was an auditor for five years in the early phases of my career. In that profession, you are always looking for errors, omissions, or weaknesses. Later in my career, I noticed that always being on the lookout for negatives had become a tendency in my thinking. After noticing that, I set about paying more attention to the positives in people and situations.

I then realized that this tendency wasn't only in me, and nor was it just because of my background in auditing. In the hypercompetitive world of business, we often give more attention to what doesn't work than what does. We generally take the good for granted and look for a bad to fix. Many of the performance evaluations I have observed in the corporate world have followed this pattern. Discussions centered on what a person does well are always more motivating and effective, yet a disproportionate amount of time can be spent talking about what needs to improve.

Deliberately seeking out the positives in people, even when it requires effort, can change the course of events and help us overcome a challenge before we even respond. This was the case with the shareholder we met earlier.

During one of our discussions, the shareholder proposed involving one of his staff members in the oversight of the business. Initially, I was concerned about agreeing to this because it would mean giving this shareholder greater access to information. Nonetheless, I was open to seeing if his staff member could contribute to improving the performance of the business. As I spent time with this individual, it became apparent that he had the skills to positively impact the business. To my mind, the benefits of those skills outweighed the potential risks from the shareholder receiving more information, so I accepted his proposal.

Ultimately, this staff member made meaningful contributions to improving the performance of the business and there was no material downside to allowing the shareholder to have access to more information. If anything, agreeing to his proposal was helpful in building trust.

The idea of minding the good can be extended to almost anything. It can mean seeing the good in a person's character, even if they come across as irritating, or it can mean recognizing the potential in a person who is struggling. The harder this is to do, the more likely we are to bring out the best in others and ourselves. It can unleash forces—including the strength of others—that we didn't know existed, helping us prevail in adversity.

OUTCOMES—SURFING IMPERMANENCE

Life is a series of ever-evolving outcomes, unfolding in a constant state of impermanence. These outcomes sometimes align with our hopes and sometimes diverge. Yet, what really matters is how we navigate—or "surf"—them.

We often simplistically judge the outcomes we experience as good or bad. We do that based on how we look at events at a fixed point in time. In reality, we don't know how they will unfold, or how we will think about them at a future point. Making judgments about them creates unnecessary emotional burdens and gets in the way of progress. That was my experience when my dreams of becoming a doctor were shattered.

It was at the tender age of sixteen that I decided to become a doctor. At that time in Türkiye, in order to gain admission into university, you first submitted a list of your preferred colleges, and then you had to take a nationwide exam. Each college had a minimum score for admission. You gained entry into the first in your priority list once you achieved its minimum admission score.

Three of my top four choices were for the medical schools of different universities. I ordered my list according to the scores they required, putting down the highest scores first. I feverishly prepared for the exam. Sadly, the score I achieved was insufficient for the first four colleges on my list. I missed out on my fourth choice—which was a medical school—by a tiny margin. So, I got into my fifth choice: The Faculty of Administrative Sciences of the Middle East Technical University (METU).

Despite my disappointment, I was consoled in the knowledge that only a tenth of the candidates made it into any program. I was also aware of the prestige of METU and the increasing popularity of business as an educational degree. All in all, I concluded, my result wasn't too bad. Others felt differently; even the head instructor who had helped prepare me for the exam said he was very disappointed. That and some comments from others started to weigh on my psyche, making me feel like my result was a failure.

The late 1970s were a tumultuous period in Türkiye. The political and civil strife of the time disrupted our lives to a point where our program couldn't start as scheduled. We were told we had to wait for a whole year to begin classes. Weighing up how best to use that year—apart from doubling down on basketball—I decided to take the college entrance exam one more time. I made the exact same choices and got exactly the same result, missing out on the same medical school by a score equivalent to a small fraction of one question.

I then decided to stop trying for medical school and enrolled at METU's Faculty of Administrative Sciences. Classes started as promised, a year later than normal. Over time, I began to enjoy the business program. By the middle of the third academic year or so, I was feeling quite positive about it. The sense of failure from not being admitted to a medical school started to dissipate. In fact, it transformed into a feeling of gratitude when I realized that I had difficulty looking at blood, and later when I had a chance to travel the world working for a wonderful company.

Impermanence—that nothing is permanent—is the only constant in life. Surfing the waves of this impermanence with the emotional burden of judgments we make about outcomes—whether realized or potential—limits the heights of our experiences. Viewing all outcomes as positive isn't the answer, either. There will always be times when the result will fall short of our hopes. A more realistic stance is to have the conviction that whatever the outcomes may be, we will always move forward constructively. That will help us surf bigger waves and let the forces of nature propel us to new heights.

A quote that is often attributed to Shams Tabrizi—the spiritual partner of Rumi—offers a helpful perspective for navigating life's constant change: "Don't fret that your life will be turned upside down; how do you know that when it does, it won't be better?"

ACCEPTING A CHALLENGE

Overcoming adversity requires both an understanding of the situation we face, and an acceptance of it, however disruptive it may have been. We have already talked about how to gain a quality understanding in chapter 6. By following the framework outlined there and making our judgments with a smart bias for positivity we put ourselves in a strong position to respond effectively. However, even the clearest understanding remains incomplete without acceptance, as true resilience begins only when we make peace with reality.

Acceptance means reaching a state of contentment—not one of passive resignation, but one that comes from acknowledging what is, and finding the strength to move forward. For some of life's tougher challenges, that is easier said than done, often requiring deep introspection and support from others.

A key to this acceptance is reconciling with the reasons behind what has happened. If the cause lies in our own actions, it means owning our mistakes and learning from them. If it stems from others—be it an honest mistake, a betrayal, or even a deliberate harm—it means coming to terms with that reality. This doesn't necessarily mean forgiving but recognizing that such failings are a part of human life. If it was simply the luck of the draw, acceptance means shifting from "Why me?" to "What can I create from this?"

The legendary tennis star Arthur Ashe once faced a fan who, when referring to his battle with AIDS, asked him: "Why did God have to select you for such a bad disease?" He responded that as one of 50 million children around the world who started playing tennis, he never asked "why me?" when he won Wimbledon. So why, now, would he ask that question when he was in pain?

Accepting what happened to us will help us *define* the challenge we are facing more clearly. While this may seem unnecessary, a clear definition and an articulation of why it is important to overcome it can be highly valuable, especially when multiple interconnected problems are involved.

The shareholder case we discussed earlier illustrates this complexity: the threat of litigation, poor business performance, frayed shareholder relations, and the precarious state of the organization—all intertwined. Our personal challenges often mirror this. Recognizing these connections enables us to define our challenge, set priorities, and tackle one manageable problem at a time.

Finally, accepting a challenge also means recognizing what it demands of our inner selves. Will overcoming it require us to exert stronger will power, understand and manage our sense of self better, become more disciplined, or think with a long-term perspective? Is it calling on us to be wiser, to forge better relationships, or to evolve our philosophy of life? Reaching a point of wanting to meet that demand of our inner selves is a defining step in overcoming adversity. It's the shot from the starting pistol that shifts our posture from defense to offense.

17

RESPOND OR REACT?

You are neither the master of your life, nor are you helpless in the face of life's challenges. [1]

—Shams Tabrizi

How much control do we really have over our lives? This question has been debated endlessly by philosophers, scientists, and theologians. The notion that our decisions may actually stem from our unconscious minds makes the answer even more elusive. This chapter's quote provides a pragmatic answer to that elusive question.

When it comes to the challenges life throws our way, much is indeed beyond our control, with external factors weighing heavily on how they develop over time. Yet, we can exercise meaningful power from the moment a challenge appears, all the way to our eventual response to it. A quote which is widely attributed to the Austrian psychiatrist and Holocaust survivor Viktor Frankl suggests: "Between the stimulus and response, there is a space and, in that space, lies our freedom and power to choose our response. In our response lies our growth and our freedom."

[1] Author's translation.

This chapter will focus on using that space in a resourceful way. The discussions in the previous chapter included elements of such resourcefulness. We will build on these here by posing three questions to help us determine whether we are using everything within our power to overcome our challenges.

The first question is whether our response is guided by a clear vision of how we emerge from adversity. A vision isn't a wish or a hope. It is a vivid image of a future we believe we can bring into existence, one that propels us with certainty. We can wield greater influence over the course of events when we are driven by such a vision.

While we talked about envisioning in the context of our legacies in chapter 8, a vision can be for anything—a meaningful relationship, a rich conversation, a good day, or how we emerge from a challenge. The concepts of the first and second creations presented there apply equally well to any of these—first envisioning desired outcomes, and then bringing that vision to life. However, when we are faced with more testing times, a unique dynamic comes into play: a new and perhaps unexpected reality, disrupting the baseline from which we project into the future.

Conceiving an aspirational vision from this new baseline requires a meaningful shift in perspective. Certain challenges naturally catalyze this shift; for instance, those enduring debilitating illnesses often report a deepened spiritual connection and a transformed outlook. These unfortunate circumstances can sometimes inspire compelling visions.

Often, perspective shifts require a conscious effort. This change begins when we *accept* the challenge we are facing—a concept we explored at the end of the previous chapter. Acceptance provides the mental space and clarity needed to begin envisioning a better future. Key to that process is to foster the belief that we hold the ability to create an aspirational new reality, regardless of the circumstances. After all, if we can create musical instruments, art, or fashion by upcycling garbage, we can always create a brighter future for ourselves, no matter the situation.

A vision of emerging stronger from adversity can serve as an inner source of inspiration as we navigate challenges. It also guides us in making choices, leading us to the second question in evaluating whether we are being resourceful in responding to a challenge: how do we make our key decisions?

Tougher challenges often come with ambiguity, uncertainty, and high stakes. The question is, in such moments, are we utilizing all of the resources available to us, especially the wisdom of our inner selves and that of our human ecosystem? We talk about this in the next section. Finally, are we acting on our decisions with fortitude? While we explored the concept of inner strength in chapter 13, here we will focus on applying it specifically to how we respond to adversity.

When faced with a challenge, reflecting and acting on these three questions will reveal to us the true extent of control we exert over our lives. This resourcefulness will help us uncover the depth and the richness in our physical, intellectual, emotional, and spiritual capacities. As a modern adaptation of the ideas in Horace's *Sermones et Epistulae* (*Satires and Epistle*) eloquently states: "Adversity reveals genius, prosperity conceals it."

CRAFTING OUR DECISIONS

Our decisions mark the turning points on our path to overcoming challenges. This idea is beautifully captured in a quote attributed to the Greek philosopher Pythagoras: "Choices are the hinges of destiny."

Decision-making is both an art and a science. The scientific part is straightforward. It is about being methodical, analytical, and rational, and involves setting specific goals, identifying options, defining criteria for evaluating those options, and conducting research and analysis. Any or all of these approaches can be helpful in making decisions.

Our bigger decisions are usually cloaked by ambiguity and uncertainty, requiring us to go beyond the rational part of decision-making. The example I shared in the previous chapter about how I ended up in my profession is of this kind. Most of us decide on our professions at an age when we know little about ourselves or the profession. To make it even more unfair, at the time we make that decision, we have no idea how we will feel about that choice at a later stage in life.

Many of the big decisions we make in our lives are similar. There are always unknowns and uncertainties in the circumstances. The greater the ambiguity in the landscape, the more the art side of decision-making can guide us toward the right choices. This idea is aptly captured by Albert Einstein in this quote from 1929: "I believe in intuitions and inspirations. I sometimes feel that I am right. I do not know that I am."

All of us have probably experienced this feeling. A decision I had to make earlier in my career vividly brought this idea home to me. I had been asked to move to a position which would have given me an experience which I had been seeking. I was told that the senior leadership of the company was highly supportive of the move. Although everything about this position looked promising, my intuition resisted it from the moment I heard the offer. I sensed that the leadership and the culture of the organization I was asked to join might somehow hinder my career progression.

I couldn't quite articulate why I felt that way, even to myself, but the inner voice was loud and clear. On the other hand, the benefits of accepting the offer were also clear: it provided the right kind of experience for me at that stage in my career and had the support of the senior leadership. Further, I didn't expect to have any issues with the financial package, so why would I not accept it?

I ended up following my intuition and declined the offer. Expecting backlash from senior leadership, I was surprised to receive none. Later on, there were other great opportunities for me to gain the experience I was looking for. Reflecting on that decision, it felt as if something within me knew better than my conscious mind and, fortunately, I listened to it.

While I don't advocate making all our tough decisions relying solely on intuition, it is important to recognize that a part of us can know the right answer without reasoning and analysis. Each of us possesses this inner knowledge. We variously call it intuition, instinct, or gut feeling. It can manifest itself in many different ways—whether as an inner conflict between our hearts and minds, a realization of the meaning behind what seems like a pure coincidence, or a sense that we don't belong in a group. Learning to trust this inner resource is a key part of the art of decision-making.

Another crucial part is connecting with the wisdom in our human ecosystem. On that front, I try to follow the Turkish maxim: "Talk with many, think with a few, and decide on your own." In a few cases, however, I allowed others to make important decisions on my behalf, and that wasn't necessarily a bad thing.

Galloping down the stairs at my İstanbul home in the early hours one summer morning, I tripped and fell. It seemed to happen in slow motion. I vividly remember trying to slow myself down by putting my right arm against the wall. That did probably slow me down, but also broke my shoulder bone. I went to the doctor that day to see what had just happened and he confirmed my suspicion. The doctor advised me that I should have it operated on. He said that if I were to decide on an operation, I shouldn't wait longer than 15–20 days, otherwise complications could arise.

I did some research and talked to people about whether I should have my shoulder operated on. As I am generally inclined toward natural solutions, I initially decided against it. I was fully aware of the downside that I could easily dislocate it again if I wasn't careful; and that if an operation were required at a later date, it would be more complicated.

On the 14th day after my fall, I had a conversation with a friend who is a doctor in a different field. He insisted that we go together to see a colleague of his who is an expert on shoulder surgeries. We went to see that doctor on the 15th day. That meeting and the words of my friend made me feel like the decision had been taken out of my hands. Luckily my sense of self didn't assert itself. So, I "decided" to go under the knife. The operation was a success. Through post-operative care, excellent coaching from my fitness instructor, and disciplined adherence to exercise, I built up my shoulder to be stronger than before the injury. In this case, it wasn't my intuition, but my human ecosystem that won the day.

Basing our decisions on intuition or on the wisdom of our human ecosystem stands in stark contrast to relying on our own reasoning and analysis. This mirrors perceived differences between the work of an artist and that of a scientist. One is methodical, analytical, and rational; the other tends to be emotional, creative, and expressive. Science develops theories about reality based on empirical evidence, whereas art expresses a reality or creates imaginative works in aesthetic and inspiring ways.

The contrasting nature of art and science need not prevent us from utilizing both approaches in decision-making. With experience, we learn which approach suits a particular context. Striking this balance will help us make our bigger, tougher decisions with more confidence, even when they are surrounded with ambiguity and uncertainty.

BUILDING INNER STRENGTH

A colleague once approached me to discuss a difficult career decision. He had been asked by a very senior person in his organization to consider a new role. Based on his description, it sounded like the position offered was only marginally better than his current one—somewhere between a lateral move and a promotion. The potential career paths in the new role didn't seem better than those in his current position. Additionally, the new role required relocation, which he was reluctant to consider.

Although he did not want to accept the offer, he was uncomfortable with the risk of saying no to a senior leader. The key question for him was: how could he decline the offer and avoid damaging his career or his relationship with this senior leader?

We first agreed that it was possible to say no and preserve—and perhaps improve—the relationship. We then worked together to identify and explore the right talking points, potential questions, and avenues the conversation could go down. After we talked about these, I sensed he was still worried by the prospect of dealing with this senior person. This trepidation would have definitely prevented him from performing at his best during the conversation. He would have likely found himself in a position many of us encounter: our preparation has been top notch, but we are unable to put the plan into action when it matters.

So, I asked him how confident he felt about the conversation he was about to have. To his credit, he openly acknowledged his worries. We talked about this and agreed that in addition to having the right talking points, he would also have to prepare himself psychologically so as to engage with his senior leader on equal terms. He took this suggestion to heart. A few weeks later, I followed up with him and learned that the conversation had gone really well. He had declined the offer, and the senior leader had praised him for the way he had done so.

While dealing with a challenging situation, we can easily skip the stage of preparing ourselves psychologically for the actions we have to take. Many obstacles can get in the way. The doubts and fears we experience in making the decision can sometimes linger while we are acting on that decision. Taking the time to prepare ourselves psychologically, just as a coach of a sports team would, is critical to overcoming a challenge. We have already talked about this preparation in chapter 13. We will introduce three additional points here.

First is preparing for others' emotional reactions. As emotions are contagious, an unexpected reaction can easily throw us off balance. Preparing ourselves for that eventuality builds our inner strength. Second is about developing self-belief. Feeling doubtful doesn't necessarily mean that we don't believe. All it means is that we still need to confront our doubts and find actionable ways to overcome them. There will always be an inner voice pointing to negative self-judgments or gloomy scenarios. In building self-belief, we can either use that negativity to strengthen our approach or put it where it belongs—the trash bin—and hit delete twice.

Finally, our human ecosystem can support us in building inner strength in many ways, with coaching being especially impactful.

I stumbled on the idea of being coached around the midpoint of my career. In the early months of a leadership role, I was told very directly by a friend—and a coach—that she thought I was struggling in my new role. She said I needed help. It wasn't easy for my sense of self to swallow that comment. After all, I had already achieved success in my career, reaching a senior position. I didn't like to hear that I needed help to do my job. While I recognized the problems in the business, I wasn't yet ready to look within myself for the reasons.

After discussions with her and some self-reflection, I accepted that change had to start with me and decided to engage her as my coach. She was very effective in holding up a mirror by asking incisive questions. On my side, I always prepared for our discussions and took the time to reflect on them afterwards. After a number of sessions, I began to make the necessary changes within myself, and, consequently, felt a lot more comfortable and effective in the role.

This process gave me ideas for how I could coach myself. I acted on these ideas and found that self-coaching can be helpful—but only up to a point. There are times when we simply cannot replicate the objectivity of an outside coach who cares about our growth. I also learned that coaching conversations aren't limited to formal sessions. If we remain open to learning, people from all age groups and backgrounds can coach us, whether they realize it or not. This is eloquently reflected in the quote we shared earlier: "When the student is ready, the teacher appears." A key part of that readiness is to make it easy for others to help us.

SHAPING OUR DESTINY

We started this chapter with one of life's existential questions: how much control do we have over our own lives? The answer to this question will remain a mystery. A quote which is often attributed to Rumi suggests that we might have more control than we realize. He says, "When you get to a point that it all feels unbearable, don't give up, that is where your destiny changes."

Adversity can test us in unforeseen ways and confront us with many factors beyond our control. Sometimes, despite our best efforts, we may just be unable to realize the outcomes we have envisioned. Yet, life is a marathon. By approaching our challenges as resourcefully as possible, we will undoubtedly build our capability and resilience and keep running with confidence. If Rumi is right, we might even be changing our destiny along the way.

18

REFLECT AND RENEW

So long as a person is capable of self-renewal, they are a living being.

—Henri-Frédéric Amiel

Extreme conditions can produce extraordinary results. Just as intense heat and pressure transform a simple element like carbon into diamonds, adversity can mold us into better versions of ourselves—a transformation which is no less remarkable. The last two chapters explored how we can achieve this growth as we navigate life's challenges. This chapter shifts focus to the critical role of reflecting on our experiences with retrospective clarity.

Looking back on difficult situations after some time has passed—with a fresh perspective, calmer emotions, and greater wisdom—offers us the opportunity to uncover profound insights. As I shared in various chapters of this book, I have often found that the limiting influence of my sense of self becomes far clearer in hindsight, usually some time after the challenge has subsided.

Here, we will delve into another potentially transformative insight about ourselves: our default modes. These default modes include the mental models, thinking habits, emotional reflexes, and biases that take over when we are faced with adversity. Because they are deeply ingrained, their influence can be hard to detect—especially when life seems to be working out well. However, becoming aware of how these default modes are holding us back can make a significant difference to our growth.

During a critical career phase, I spent four years working under a senior leader with a reputation for being very tough. My difficulties started on day one. When I introduced myself, I received a less than warm welcome, but I thought that was just his way, and I didn't let it stress me out. Then, I made a disastrous first presentation to him. The poor results I presented and his open and strong disagreement with some of my judgments made for a terrible start.

Shortly afterwards, the business began to improve but my relationship with him didn't. Most presentations I made, even those demonstrating good results, received a skeptical reception. For most of those four years, I felt as if I was on the brink of losing my job any day, something I had never felt up to that point in my career.

Through intense focus and with a favorable macroeconomic environment, the unit I led consistently delivered strong results. Toward the end of that four-year period, these strong results helped improve the relationship. At last, I felt I had overcome this challenge.

Looking back on this years later, I noticed how my default mode had helped me solve my problem, but I had missed opportunities for growth. It's also clear that luck was on my side.

My default mode was to focus on delivering strong results, assuming that would make the problem go away. While that ultimately worked, I am not so sure it would have been so effective had the macroeconomic environment been unfavorable. In addition, having to perform in such a climate for four years was a sign that there were issues I couldn't overcome.

On reflection, I was able to spot a number of gaps in the way I read and responded to that challenge. I don't think I understood why that senior leader kept being so difficult, even when results improved. Neither did I take the time to understand the "inside story" in any depth, i.e., what was going on inside my head and how I could deal with that. In other words, I wasn't sufficiently introspective.

My vision was only about the "outside story," i.e., the results. Yet even that was incomplete as I hadn't developed a vision for improving the relationship. Finally, I did not reach out to my human ecosystem for help during those difficult four years. This was a clear case of my default mode being effective for that specific challenge, but I was missing opportunities for growth.

Reflecting on our toughest challenges after some time has passed can reveal key insights. By evaluating how we read and responded to a particular challenge, we can uncover vital truths about ourselves and our growth.

This habit can do even more for us. Over time, the awareness we gain through these "look-backs" helps us anticipate how our default modes drive us, allowing us to "hack" them before they cause any harm. The first time I can remember doing this, I wasn't thinking about it as hacking my default mode—but in essence, that's exactly what I was doing.

Earlier in my career I transitioned from a financial role into a general management position. In my financial role, I always carried a big briefcase around with me filled with all the information I could possibly need. That wasn't only because of the limited technology in comparison with today; it also came from my desire to always be on top of the financial details in case I was ever questioned on them.

Thinking about my new role, I realized that such a desire for control would make me ineffective. While that sounds logical, acting on that realization didn't come easily. By the time of that promotion, I had already worked 15 years in positions where I could exercise significant levels of control over my work. Fortunately, I was able to hack that default mode and became a lot more selective with the information I carried around with me. I even downsized my briefcase, despite the expanded role.

That hacking not only improved my performance as a general manager, it also helped me better manage increasing responsibilities. I kept augmenting my capacity by changing the way I worked, and technology made that task even easier.

A similar opportunity came about when I moved from a field role to one in headquarters. Among the most important differences between the two roles were the speed at which decisions were made and the visibility of one's impact. In my field role, I was drawing a great deal of motivation from those two sources. Anticipating how the loss of these might feed into the way I dealt with the headquarters role, I prepared myself to draw similar satisfaction from different sources.

The two roles never felt the same. Yet that preparation helped me find fulfillment in working with a new group of stakeholders, providing a different perspective on the organization and its ecosystem.

I observed the positive effects of hacking that default mode as I embarked on a new phase in my professional life. It then became second nature to step back and reflect deeply on why I cared for a certain business or a social impact opportunity, strengthening my engagement in whatever direction I chose to pursue.

Hacking our default modes is like releasing a new version of our mind's operating system. Just as updates to iOS or Android improve the performance of our devices, each adjustment to our default settings makes us more efficient, effective, and better equipped for growth.

In the defense game of life, we dance to an endless playlist of challenges that continually push us out of our comfort zones. Each song on this playlist is an invitation to create a new version of ourselves—wiser, more open to love, more skilled, and better equipped to cope with life's complexities. Embracing adversity with a growth mindset dignifies and beautifies our dance, producing versions of ourselves we might have never imagined.

GROW FOREVER

19

DISCOVERING INFINITY

***Be not afraid of growing slowly,
be afraid only of standing still.***

—Chinese proverb

Our life as we know it begins somewhere on Planet Earth, at a fixed point in time, and lasts for an unknown period. We start out as 4-D beings, equipped to experience the world physically, intellectually, emotionally, and spiritually. As we develop, we gain a sense of self and become aware of our will and conscience.

Over the course of our lives, we assume many roles, transitioning from that of a student to a professional, entrepreneur, leader, artist, or a public servant. We play the roles of a parent, a partner, or a citizen. In these and other roles we take on, we face an endless flow of challenges, experiencing joys and sorrows, hopes and fears, victories and defeats. Through this magnificent journey, we continually uncover the richness within ourselves.

Soulgery is about accelerating the pace of this discovery and unlocking more of our potential as a natural part of our experiences. We achieve this by applying the 4 Acts of Growth to real life—whether in pursuing our aspirations or navigating challenges. The 4 Acts offer a framework for understanding the self and one's life, which, when put into practice, accelerates our growth. They are grounded in four core beliefs:

1. Sourcing inspiration from life.
2. Focusing first on the impact we make.
3. Striving for performance excellence in all life roles.
4. Leveraging life's challenges for growth.

As we proposed throughout this book, embracing the 4 Acts enriches our human equities of love, wisdom, and character, and develops our core skills. These, in turn, enable us to make a profound impact in our roles, creating an echo that fuels a virtuous cycle of growth and impact.

Applying the 4 Acts involves a deep level of introspection, spanning various areas of personal growth. Appendix 2 presents a list of these areas—everything discussed in this book—that require quality time for self-reflection. Understandably, this list of 19 focus areas may feel a bit overwhelming.

It is important to note that applying Soulgery is a gradual process that unfolds at your own pace. Focusing on a manageable number of areas will make this process most effective. Rest assured, the benefits will be felt with each step along the way. We are free to choose where to start based on what we believe will be most helpful in the context of our own lives. Each of us will progress at our own pace, making this journey uniquely ours.

We can start with a specific part of an Act of Growth or select as many areas as we feel ready to tackle. This starting point might be a philosophical quest, such as the search for meaning, or a practical endeavor such as implementing a personal planning system. It could involve a legacy we wish to create in our professional roles. As life constantly confronts us with adversity, we may choose to experiment with ideas presented in Act 4—Hack Your Growth. Alternatively, we can begin by developing a number of skills such as managing our psyche, listening, simplifying, or decision-making.

Once we have gained a sufficient level of comfort in the areas we have focused on, we can progress to other parts of the Soulgery model, continuing this process until we feel we have internalized everything that we find helpful. In summary, there is no single right way to approach this journey—only the path that aligns best with our personal needs and goals.

Our sense of self plays a catalytic role in our growth. In chapter 5, we discussed how managing its inhibiting influence opens our hearts to love. This also broadens and deepens our wisdom, as we experience life without the haze of self-serving motives. In addition, we become better observers of the human qualities which bond us with one another. The human equities of love, wisdom, and character naturally enhance our skills across our careers, relationships, or any role we take on. Given this foundational effect on our growth, staying mindful of the inhibiting influence of the sense of self will accelerate our progress, no matter which area we work on.

Finally, two points are worth highlighting. First, it is helpful to revisit different parts of Soulgery from time to time. What might not feel relevant today could resonate at another point, as our lives are in constant flux.

Second, while Soulgery emphasizes working on ourselves, accelerating our growth is far from a solo mission. Our human ecosystem also plays a critical role, as we discussed throughout the book. Meaningful conversations with those we trust help us learn more about ourselves, others, and life itself. In pursuing our potential, *we* will always surpass *me*.

STEWARDING OUR JOURNEY

This lifelong journey of growth requires someone to guide our course, evaluate our progress, and adjust as needed. That role belongs to none other than ourselves. It's up to each of us to determine our road map and how we choose to steward our own journey. In order to help in developing this road map, I briefly share below how I have been stewarding my own. As with the other practices I have shared earlier, the intent is to serve thought starters, not to propose a specific solution.

Let's return to the salt cedar moment in chapter 1. Years of questioning my life's ultimate goal led me to conclude that it was to discover my potential as a human being—not just as a business professional or leader. As I became convinced that managing the influence of my sense of self was central to my lifelong growth journey, it became my primary focus. The stories shared throughout this book have only reinforced my belief that this should remain a priority for the rest of my life.

Following those initial years, I started adding new growth areas, influenced by the demands of my role as a business executive and leader. These included gaining wisdom in politics, economics, social issues, as well as expanding my understanding of technological developments and global affairs. At times, I focused on honing specific skills like asking incisive questions, active listening, and decision-making. I even set goals for improving my emotional responses when dealing with certain personalities.

Over the years, my curiosity drove me to explore psychology, spirituality, and life's existential questions more deeply. Nurturing my well-being has also remained a top priority. All the while, I maintained the discipline of managing my own performance, setting growth goals, and evaluating myself objectively—always seeking to align with the rhythm that makes me most effective.

I continue to be fascinated by the persistence of the impulse to serve my sense of self and its subtle manifestation. One of my recent discoveries is what I call, "treating my previous selves with disdain" syndrome. When I view my current self as superior to my past self, I start to pity who I was—a clear sign that I am glorifying my current self. As was the case in the other examples I shared earlier, becoming aware of this limiting thought has allowed me to manage it better.

Eddie Robinson, who is recognized as one of the greatest American football coaches of all time, famously said, "Coaching is a profession of love. You can't coach people unless you love them." Stewarding our lifelong journey of growth is like coaching ourselves; it is also a labor of love—*for the self.*

Self-love involves accepting ourselves unconditionally, while continually striving to move forward. Self-love leads to high standards but avoids harsh self-judgment when we fall short, or excessive admiration when we succeed.

Above all, it means being kind to ourselves. This journey is full of frustrations, at not being able to overcome problems no matter how hard we try, or at missing opportunities. If we react by being too tough on ourselves or dwelling on regrets, we aren't showing self-love. Self-love helps us embrace the journey as it is and keeps us moving forward with grace, resolve, and hope, regardless of the outcomes.

An Invitation

That old salt cedar stands strong and beautiful, even after two decades. Sitting under it, as I reflect on my growth experience, a quote that is attributed to Rumi comes to mind: "I learned that every mortal will taste death, but only some will taste life." To me, this taste of life is about experiencing ever more of my physical, intellectual, emotional, and spiritual faculties. It is about enjoying a sense of wholeness, both within myself and with the greater systems I inhabit. I call this a full human experience.

Whether I am among the "some" that Rumi refers to or not, the memories of moments that felt like that full human experience push me forward. I need no convincing that the joy of this journey is what truly matters to me.

Knowing that joy multiplies when shared, I want to extend a heartfelt invitation to you—to unleash your true potential, create lasting legacies, rise above your challenges, and experience the same joy of growth. By accepting this invitation, you will not only transform your own life, but also uplift and inspire those around you, creating ripples that reach far beyond.

These ripple effects are akin to the *butterfly effect* in Chaos Theory, which suggests that seemingly insignificant events can have unpredictable and far-reaching consequences—like the flapping of a butterfly's wings in one part of the world influencing the weather patterns in another. Our growth creates a unifying effect in whatever role we play, starting with our inner circles, extending to other parts of our human ecosystem, and perhaps even beyond.

Just like the scientist's son assembling the map of the world by piecing together the human being—as we presented at the end of chapter 2—our collective efforts in growth will weave together the world, one person at a time. This ambitious vision, compared to what is called a moonshot in our day, is more like an Ursa shot—aiming not for the nearest celestial body, but for the farthest galaxy from Earth.

We really don't know whether we can collectively achieve this Ursa shot, but we do know that by embarking on this journey with the vision of weaving the world together, one person at a time, we will discover our greater selves along the way.

Take the first step today and embrace the adventure that lies ahead.

APPENDIX 1

CORE SKILLS FOR SOULGERY

This appendix summarizes the skills we can build by undertaking the 4 Acts.[1] These skills have broad relevance, both within the context of the 4 Acts and beyond. The references to specific Acts of Growth aren't meant to capture the entire scope of a skill's application. For example, we talk about the skill of simplification in the context of managing our time, but that skill can also be important for other purposes. Likewise, we talk about decision-making in the context of responding to our challenges, but that skill also has much broader relevance.

GROUP 1: MANAGING OUR PSYCHE

This group includes the skills to:

- Become aware of our thoughts, emotions, and ways of thinking,
- Evaluate our thoughts, emotions, and ways of thinking,
- Change our thoughts and ways of thinking,

[1]The definitions provided for these skills are simply my best attempt at expressing my own conceptualization, for the specific purpose of undertaking the 4 Acts. Furthermore, the discussion in the 4 Acts about these skills focuses only on a few areas which I believe make the most important difference in building that skill. If the readers feel the need for a more comprehensive training in them, they are encouraged to do so.

- Channel our emotions to a useful purpose,
- Connect with something bigger than the self and lose our sense of separateness.

The 4 Acts connect with this skill group in many different ways. Some of them are as follows:

- **Act 1:** Managing one's sense of self. This concept is first introduced in chapters 1 and 3. Chapter 5 proposes a way of carrying it out.
- **Act 2:** Chapter 8 contains a discussion on leveraging our doubts to strengthen our belief. Chapter 9 talks about recognizing and embracing human qualities which bond us.
- **Act 3:** Chapter 14 discusses managing our emotions and opening ourselves to spiritual engagement.
- **Act 4:** The four chapters discussing this act talk about evaluating our judgments, understanding and accepting what a challenge demands from our inner selves, building inner strength in responding to our challenges, and becoming more aware of and "hacking" our default modes.

GROUP 2: COGNITIVE SKILLS

Systems thinking: The ability to think holistically and deeply; discussed in chapter 6, in the section titled: "A Quality Understanding."

Philosophical thinking: The ability to think philosophically. Chapter 4 talks about it in the discussion of a search for meaning. Chapter 9 talks about the philosophical foundations of the human qualities which are part of our character.

Character perception: The ability to spot the human qualities in one's character is discussed in chapter 9.

Simplification: The ability to capture the essence of issues and to eliminate clutter. It is discussed in chapter 12, in the section titled: "Simplifying."

Associating: The ability to see similarities, patterns, or themes in seemingly unrelated events, discussed in chapter 6, in the section titled: "Unraveling Life's Causalities."

Zooming out: The ability to elevate our vantage point, also discussed in chapter 6, in the section titled: "Unraveling Life's Causalities."

GROUP 3: ACTIVITY SKILLS

Listening: Discussed in chapter 6 in the section titled: "A Quality Understanding."

Asking questions: Discussed in chapter 6 in the section titled: "A Quality Understanding."

Decision-making: Discussed in chapter 17 in the section titled: "Crafting our Decisions."

Communicating: Discussed in chapter 13, as part of preparing ourselves to communicate from the heart.

Problem solving: This is a key skill which isn't explicitly discussed, except that the entire Act 4 can be thought of as a problem-solving exercise.

GROUP 4: ADVANCED GROWTH SKILLS

Envisioning: The ability to conceive aspirational visions for our future. It is covered in chapter 8 in terms of creating legacies and in the introductory section of chapter 17.

Augmenting our capacity: The ability to change ways of working in order to do increasingly impactful work. We discuss an example of this in chapter 18, where we talk about hacking our default mode.

Agility: The ability to adapt to changing contexts. An example of this is also in chapter 18, where discuss hacking our default mode.

APPENDIX 2

SUMMARY OF FOCUS AREAS

1. Developing a personal philosophy
2. Opening your heart
3. Pursuing deeper understanding
4. Maintaining your humility
5. Cultivating curiosity
6. Unraveling life's causalities
7. Embracing a legacy mindset
8. Shaping your character
9. Personal planning
10. Tracking time
11. Simplifying your life
12. Evolving the way you operate
13. Preparing to perform with excellence
14. Owning your well-being
15. Managing your emotions

16. Connecting with spirituality
17. Reading challenges constructively
18. Sharpening your decision-making
19. Hacking your default mode

ABOUT THE AUTHOR

Ahmet Bozer is a global business leader with a distinguished career spanning over 30 years. During his tenure at the Coca-Cola Company, he served in many senior leadership roles, including as president of the Eurasia and Africa Group and president of Coca-Cola International. Working across continents and cultures, he developed a passion for unlocking potential—both in his teams and within himself—gaining profound insights into personal and professional growth.

Following his corporate career, Ahmet became involved in nonexecutive roles in businesses, NGOs, and academia, as well as in philanthropy, mentoring, and entrepreneurial ventures. These experiences deepened his understanding of individual potential and fueled his desire to share the lessons from his journey to benefit others. Since retiring from the Coca-Cola Company in 2016, he has devoted himself to developing *Soulgery*.

Having lived and worked extensively in both Türkiye and the United States, Ahmet's life reflects the interplay of collectivist and individualist cultures. This dual perspective inspired him to integrate the best of both worlds into his approach. His quest for meaning has been deeply influenced by Sufi philosophy. Along this journey, he came to understand that the essence of the Sufi path—raising consciousness through awareness and reflection—is also pivotal to fostering growth. Embracing this timeless wisdom, he made it the core of *Soulgery*.

With his extensive leadership experience and decades-long dedication to *Soulgery*, Ahmet is uniquely positioned to present this distinctive model—one that bridges the practical and philosophical while seamlessly blending Eastern and Western wisdom.

Printed in Dunstable, United Kingdom

81781395R00099